I0039521

The Genealogist's Guide to Researching Tax Records

Carol Cooke Darrow, CG
and
Susan Winchester, Ph.D., C.P.A.

HERITAGE BOOKS
2007

HERITAGE BOOKS
AN IMPRINT OF HERITAGE BOOKS, INC.

Books, CDs, and more—Worldwide

For our listing of thousands of titles see our website
at
www.HeritageBooks.com

Published 2007 by
HERITAGE BOOKS, INC.
Publishing Division
65 East Main Street
Westminster, Maryland 21157-5026

Copyright © 2007 Carol Cooke Darrow, CG and
Susan Winchester, Ph.D., C.P.A.

All rights reserved. No part of this book may be reproduced or
transmitted in any form or by any means, electronic or mechanical,
including photocopying, recording or by any information storage
and retrieval system without written permission from the author,
except for the inclusion of brief quotations in a review.

International Standard Book Number: 978-0-7884-4298-8

For all the genealogists who spend hours looking at microfilm in hopes of locating their ancestors.

Table of Contents

LIST OF FIGURES ix

LIST OF TABLES xi

PREFACE xiii

CHAPTER 1. GETTING STARTED IN TAX RECORDS 1

BENEFITS OF TAX RECORD RESEARCH 2
RESEARCH CAN BE TEDIOUS – UNTIL YOU SUCCEED 3
TAX PROCESS 4
LOCATING TAX RECORDS 8
RESEARCH TAX RECORDS AT COURTHOUSE OR ARCHIVE 10
TAX RECORDS AS SUBSTITUTES FOR CENSUS RECORDS 11
VERIFY COUNTY FORMATION DATE 12
FOLLOWING THE RECORDS YEAR BY YEAR 13
ISOLATED RECORDS 13
INDEXES: NEVER THE FINAL ANSWER 15
A WORD ABOUT SLAVES 16
FINDING THE RIGHT RECORD IN THE WRONG PLACE 17
READY TO BEGIN? 17

CHAPTER 2. RESEARCH TECHNIQUES 19

TYPES OF TAXES 19
TAX RECORDS MAY BE COMBINED 20
HOW TO APPROACH A TAX RECORD 20
IDENTIFY INFORMATION BEING COLLECTED 23
SOURCES FOR INTERPRETING TAX INFORMATION 24
CONSIDER SPELLING VARIATIONS 24
BECOME FAMILIAR WITH NOTATIONS AND ABBREVIATIONS 25
  *Research Example: Separate Men with the Same Name in the Same
  County* 27
DOING THE MATH 28
  Research Example: Estimate Wealth of An Ancestor 29
RECORDS THAT REPORT ONLY ASSESSED VALUE 31
PAYING TAXES IN THE COIN OF THE REALM 33
CALCULATING WITH POUNDS, SHILLINGS, AND PENCE 34

Research Example: Estimate Wealth of an Ancestor 35
FORMING A HYPOTHESIS...36
SUMMARY OF RESEARCH TECHNIQUES..38

CHAPTER 3. POLL TAXES **41**

TAXES "BY THE POLL" WERE EARLIEST AMERICAN TAXES...............42
MASSACHUSETTS POLL TAX, 1646...43
VIRGINIA TITHABLES...44
THE TITHABLE PROCESS 46
POLL BOOKS AND VOTING RIGHTS 47
Research Example: Locate an Ancestor in a Specific County.........50
HEAD TAXES IN OTHER COLONIES 51
Research Example: Separate Men with the Same Name in the Same County...53
TRACKING CHANGES THROUGH TAX LISTS OVER TIME....................56
Research Example: Identify Men as They Become Adults 57
FINDING THE LANDLESS ANCESTOR 57
Research Example: Research A Landless Ancestor.......................57
POLL TAX RECORDS CAN REPLACE THE CENSUS 59

CHAPTER 4. LAND TAXES...**63**

COLONIAL LAND DISTRIBUTION 63
LAND TAXES AFTER THE REVOLUTION..67
TAX EXEMPTIONS USED TO ENCOURAGE SETTLEMENT.....................67
TAX RECORDS CAN IDENTIFY THE LAND AND LOCATION..................69
Research Example: Separate Men with the Same Name in the Same County...70
Research Example: Use Tax Information to Lead to Other Valuable Records 72
DELINQUENT LAND TAX SALES..73
TRACKING DELINQUENT LAND TAX SALES RECORDS 74
LAND TAX RECORDS CAN POINT TO A MIGRATION TRAIL 75
LAND HOLDINGS MAY IMPLY ARRIVAL DATE 76
TAX LEDGERS ARRANGED BY LEGAL LAND DESCRIPTION.................77
ADDITIONAL INFORMATION COLLECTED IN TAX RECORDS...............78
INFORMATION COMMON TO LAND TAX RECORDS 79

CHAPTER 5. PERSONAL PROPERTY TAXES...............................**81**

PAYING FOR GOVERNMENT 81
ESTATES ARE TAXABLE..83

Research Example: Establish a Year of Death As Estate Becomes Taxable..84
LAND AND PERSONAL PROPERTY TAX LISTS COMBINED.....................85
Research Example: Estimate Wealth of An Ancestor....................86
PROPERTY TAX LISTS EXPANDED OVER TIME.....................................87
STATE INCOME TAX REPLACES SOME PERSONAL PROPERTY TAXES...89
HOMESTEAD EXEMPTIONS ENACTED...90
PERSONAL PROPERTY TAX—"EVERYMAN" TAX..................................91

CHAPTER 6. FEDERAL TAXES..93

DIRECT TAX OF 1798..94
TARIFFS AND IMPORT DUTIES...99
DIRECT TAXES OF 1813, 1815, AND 1816..100
DIRECT TAX OF 1861...100
FEDERAL INCOME TAXES (1862-1872)..104
CONFEDERATE TAXES..106
TARIFFS DECLINE IN SIGNIFICANCE...109
INCOME TAX RECONSIDERED...109
TAX PROTESTS..110
TAX ASSESSORS AND COLLECTORS..113

CHAPTER 7. INHERITANCE AND ESTATE TAXES...............................117

FEDERAL ESTATE AND INHERITANCE TAXES.......................................118
STATE ESTATE AND INHERITANCE TAXES...119
Research Example: Identify the Heirs of an Estate.....................123
ESTATE AND INHERITANCE TAXES CAN PROVE RELATIONSHIPS.......126

CHAPTER 8. MISCELLANEOUS TAX RECORDS....................................127

MILITIA SERVICE...127
ROAD ORDERS..130
ECCLESIASTICAL TAXES...132
FACULTY TAXES..133
BUSINESS LICENSES..133
LIQUOR TAXES..134
SCHOOL TAXES...135
FEDERAL HEAD TAX ON ALIENS...135
OLD AGE ASSISTANCE TAX...136

CHAPTER 9. SUMMARY..141

SUMMARY OF RESEARCH TECHNIQUES...142

APPENDIX A TEXTURAL RECORDS OF THE DIRECT TAX
COMMISSION IN THE SOUTHERN STATES..145

APPENDIX B MICROFILMED RECORDS OF THE INTERNAL
REVENUE ASSESSMENT LISTS, 1862-1874..149

APPENDIX C STATE INHERITANCE TAX LAWS THROUGH 1913 ..151

APPENDIX D STATE OLD AGE ASSISTANCE LAWS, AS OF 1934 153

GLOSSARY..155

RESEARCH BIBLIOGRAPHY 157

BIBLIOGRAPHY OF SELECTED TAX RECORDS 162

INDEX..165

List of Figures

Fig. 1. A List of Tythables in Fairfax County, Virginia, 1762. 4

Fig. 2. Assessment page of the Fifteenth Eighteen-Penny Provincial Tax, 13 March 1772, for the City & County of Philadelphia 6

Fig. 3. Orange County, Virginia, Defaulters List, 1738 7

Fig. 4. New York City Assessment Roll, 1807 14

Fig. 5. Petition of Matthew Blanckenbücker to be excused from taxes 45

Fig. 6. Index for Cook/Cooke entries in *Amelia County, Virginia, Tax Lists, 1736-1764: An Every Name Index* 53

Fig. 7. Amelia County, Virginia, Tithable List, 1756 55

Fig. 8. List of properties for sale for delinquent taxes, Golden City, Colorado Territory, 1868 74

Fig. 9. Polk County, Tennessee, Real Estate Tax List, 1894 76

Fig. 10. Homestead exemption petition of C.I. Cooke, Carroll County, Georgia, 1883 90

Fig. 11. Form A, Direct Tax of 1798, Franklin County, Pennsylvania 97

Fig. 12. Confederate tax notice, Orange County, North Carolina, 1864 108

Fig. 13. Notice of military poll tax, Colorado Territory, 1873 129

Fig. 14. Road Order, Amelia County, Virginia, 1771 131

Fig. 15. Alien Certificate, Federal Head Tax on Aliens, 1918 136

List of Tables

Table 1. Stone Family Tax Record, North Carolina, 1815 27

Table 2. Tennessee Tax List, 1833 29

Table 3. Georgia Tax Digest, Fayette County, 1828 31

Table 4. Pennsylvania Provincial Tax, 1772 32

Table 5. Massachusetts Town Tax Collection, 1773 35

Table 6. Tithable List, Surry County, Virginia, 1699 45

Table 7. Selected Tithables, Orange County, Virginia, 1739 50

Table 8. Study of John Cook Family Tithables, Amelia County,
Virginia, 1754-1763 56

Table 9. Tax List, Westmoreland County, Pennsylvania, 1783 71

Table 10. Tax List, Westmoreland County, Pennsylvania, 1787 ...72

Table 11. Headright Categories in Texas 77

Table 12. Personal Property Tax List, Gloucester County,
Virginia, 1782 82

Table 13. Tax Study of Charnock Rust, Maury County,
Tennessee, 1837-1842 84

Table 14. Assessment List, Cumberland County,
Pennsylvania, 1817 85

Table 15. Tax List, Campbell County, Kentucky, 1795 86

Table 16. Some Records of the Direct Tax of 1798 98

Table 17. Selected Internal Revenue Tax Assessments,
Colorado Territory, 1863 105

Table 18. Selected Internal Revenue Tax Assessments,
Georgia Division 4, 1866 106

Table 19. Record of Estates Subject to Collateral Inheritance
Tax, New Jersey, 1912 121

Table 20. Personal Property List for Estate of Irving S. Morse....124

Table 21. Distribution of Estate of Irving S. Morse 125

Preface

Everyone pays taxes in one form or another, thereby creating records. Those records can establish your location, real estate, personal possessions, economic status, and perhaps even occupation and family relationships. The challenge for genealogists is to locate the records that will reveal the same information about their ancestors. Why then are these records among the most underutilized by even experienced researchers?

There are a number of reasons. Just as there was no single procedure for levying or collecting taxes, there is no single procedure for studying tax records. Any level of government could impose a tax so you may find records at the federal, state or colony, county, and even city governments. The types of taxes levied changed frequently as did the definition of taxable property and the recording procedures for those tax records. In addition, tax records are handwritten and sometimes in poor condition.

But census records present most of the same problems. Each decade brought changes to the types of information collected and the forms on which the information was recorded. Instructions to census takers changed with each decade and influenced the resulting records. Census records are also handwritten, adding another obstacle to the research. Yet genealogists use census records as the basis for all their research. We believe that research into tax records can be just as important.

We decided to write a book that would explain some of the history behind tax records and some of the common forms and procedures used to collect taxes. We have attempted to discuss a variety of tax records and offer research techniques that will allow you to use these records effectively.

You can use tax records simply as a census to confirm an ancestor's location in a specific year. By comparing tax records for the same individual in two different locations, you may be able to determine a migration path and year of relocation. As you locate tax records for your ancestor, you can analyze the possessions being taxed and begin to make comparisons between your ancestor and his neighbors. Tax records may also help to identify and separate men with the same surname living in the same county. Most importantly, after you have studied the available information, you will be able to continue your research in other records based on the information gathered from studying tax records.

We hope you will find this book helpful on whatever level you choose to research. We believe you will be richly rewarded for your effort in learning about tax records that can reveal so much information about the life of your ancestor.

Carol Cooke Darrow, CG
Susan Winchester, Ph.D., CPA

Chapter 1. Getting Started In Tax Records

In this world nothing can be said to be certain except death and taxes.

Benjamin Franklin in a letter, 13 November 1789

Taxes are as old as civilization. As long as there have been governments, there has been a need to finance them. Tax collectors are depicted in Egyptian tomb paintings dating from 2000 B.C. Ancient Rome had an elaborate tax system that included sales taxes, inheritance taxes, and taxes on imports and exports. Over the centuries, European governments experimented with poll taxes, hearth and window taxes, excise taxes, and income taxes. The United States has experimented with a wide variety of taxes taken from these early models.

Tax records exist for much of the recorded history of America and are some of the most valuable genealogical documents. They record who paid taxes and, equally important, who did not. But the variety of taxes imposed, the constant changes in record-keeping, the task of understanding columns of numbers, and the difficulty of locating records may discourage even a dedicated genealogist.

But let's look at tax records in a little different light. Think of a tax roll or tax digest as an annual census, usually alphabetized by the first letter of the surname, which includes the number of adult males in the household, the land designation, number of acres owned, and the value of the taxable property owned by your ancestor. Wouldn't you be interested in studying such a record?

Benefits of Tax Record Research

Researchers who comb through tax records have been richly rewarded. They have discovered, as you can, that tax records may help you:

- Locate an ancestor in a specific place at a specific time.
- Track an ancestor's movement from one location to another.
- Narrow the time period during which an individual first established his residence in a specific location.
- Confirm land ownership and acres owned.
- Gather information about a landless ancestor.
- Separate men with the same name in the same county.
- Identify men as they reach adulthood and are taxed in their own right.
- Establish an ancestor's approximate year of death based on the year in which his estate appeared in the tax rolls.
- Estimate the wealth of an ancestor based on his taxable property.
- Use the information found in tax records to lead to other valuable records.

If tax records offer such rich benefits, why aren't they more widely known and used by genealogists? There are some drawbacks:

- Tax records are handwritten and sometimes difficult to read.
- The information is recorded in columns that may not be labeled or easily deciphered. You may have to do further research to understand what information was being collected.
- Research into tax records is very time-consuming. These annual records are not indexed and may cover several years.
- Records may be difficult to locate.

Research Can Be Tedious – Until You Succeed

Research is sometimes tedious—until you find just what you've been looking for. Here are some tips to make it less tedious and more rewarding.

- Gather the basic information about your ancestor's location and movements into and across the United States using available census records. Create a timeline supported by census records or census substitutes to place him in a specific state and county at the ten-year census intervals.
- Check the formation dates of the counties in which you are researching. Were they established counties at the time your ancestor was living in the area? If not, you will need to start your research in the county *as it was identified when your ancestor lived there.*
- Check the availability of records including microfilmed tax records from the Family History Library in Salt Lake City, Utah, or a local archive for that time and place.

Tax Process

Before you start your research, it's important to understand the tax process and the documents it created. The **first step** in this process was to compile a list of taxpayers and their taxable property. In the earliest colonial period the head of the household was required to submit a list of his taxable property. For example,

George Washington. **House Servants:** Thoms Bishop, Breechy, Schomberg, Jack, Doll, Jenny, Betty, Phillis, Moll, Sall, Kate. **Carpenters:** Turner Crump, Anthony, Will, Morris, George, Michael, Tom, Sam, Ned. **Smiths:** Peter, London. **Miller:** George. **Ditcher:** Robt Haims. **Home House:** Burgs Mitchell, Jack, Jack, Jack, Ned, James, Charles, Davy. **Dogue Run:** John Alton, Peros, Will, Caesar, Troy, Stafford, Betty, Sarah, Sue, Lucy. **Creek Plann:** Josiah Cook, Matt, Cupid, Will, Jenny, Kitty. **Muddy Hole:** Edwd Violette, Grig, Will, Jupiter, Essex, Sam, Betty, Ruth, Hannah, Kate, Phoebe. **River Plann:** Saml Johnson, Tom, Ben, George, Robin, Nat, Peg, Murria, Cloe, Flora, Doll. In all – 71.

Fig. 1. A List of Tythables in Fairfax County – given unto Capt. Daniel McCarty – June 9th 1762. (Bold type added for emphasis) Source: The Papers of George Washington, Colonial Series, Vol. 7, January 1761-June 1767, W.W Abbot and Dora Twohig, editors. Charlottesville: University Press of Virginia, 1990, p. 139. Reprinted with permission of the University of Virginia Press.

in Virginia the head of the household submitted a list of his tithables—the taxable individuals for whom he would pay the tax.

In colonial Massachusetts the head of each household submitted a list of his personal and real property, which was then copied into the tax books. In colonial Maryland and South Carolina landowners were required to submit information about the number of acres of land they owned as well as a memorial, that is, a statement identifying former owners and how and when the current owner came into possession of the land. A few of these original lists are available in loose records in the tax office or in personal documents in a manuscript collection.

The **second step** was to value the property in order to calculate the tax. Most of the tax records you will find are assessment records, that is, lists of assets, the value of the assets, and sometimes the tax due on those assets. In New England and the Middle Atlantic colonies tax assessors viewed the land, dwellings, and livestock and rated the property. The assessment list in Fig. 2 for the City and County of Philadelphia, Pennsylvania, for 1772 shows the actual value of the property next to its description and the assessed value in the next column. The southern colonies did not use assessors to rate the value of property because tithables were flat taxes based on the number of taxable individuals in the household. There was, however, a sort of public assessment process as tithable lists were posted in a public place where neighbors could inspect the lists and identify any irregularities such as unlisted slaves.

The **third step** was to collect the tax. Although there are few actual records of taxes paid because these receipts were given to the individual taxpayer, you will sometimes see assessment records with check marks or other indications that the tax due was actually paid. You may also find two tax lists for the same year — an assessment list and a collection list.

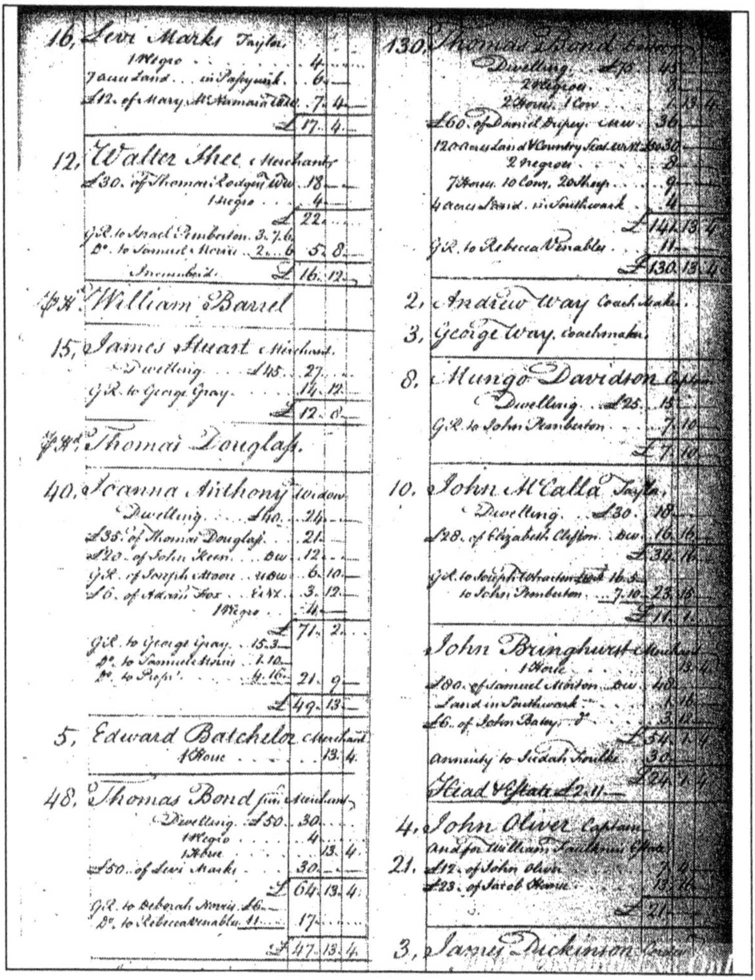
16, Levi Marks Taylor
1 Negro . . 4
7 acres Land . . in Passyunk . 6
£12. of Mary McNamara . 7. 4
£ 17. 4

12, Walter Shee Merchant
£30. of Thomas Rodgers . 18
1 Negro . 4
£ 22
G.R. to Israel Pemberton 3. 7. 6
D°. to Samuel Morris . 2. . 6 . 5. 8
£ 16. 12

William Barrel

15, James Stuart Merchant
Dwelling . £45 . 27
G.R. to George Gray . 14. 12
£ 12. 8

Thomas Douglass

40, Joanna Anthony Widow
Dwelling . £40 . 24
£35. of Thomas Douglass . 21
£20. of John Keen . 12
£6. of Adam Fox . 3. 12
1 Negro . 4
£ 71. 2
G.R. to George Gray . 15. 3
D°. to Samuel Morris . 1. 10
D°. to Props. . 4. 16 . 21. 9
£ 49. 13

5, Edward Batchelor Merchant
1 Horse . 13. 4

48, Thomas Bond jun. Merchant
Dwelling . £50 . 30
1 Negro . 4
1 Horse . 13. 4
£50. of Levi Marks . 30
£ 64. 13. 4
G.R. to Deborah Morris £6
D°. to Rebecca Venables 11 . 17
£ 47. 13. 4

130, Thomas Bond
Dwelling . £75 . 45
2 Negroes . 8
2 Horses. 1 Cow . 1. 13. 4
£60. of Daniel Dupuy . 36
120 Acres Land & Country Seat . 30
2 Negroes . 8
7 Horses. 10 Cows. 20 Sheep . 9
4 acres Land . in Southwark . 4
£ 141. 13. 4
G.R. to Rebecca Venables . 11
£ 130. 13. 4

2, Andrew Way Coach Maker
3, George Way, Coachmaker

8, Mungo Davidson Captain
Dwelling . £25 . 15
G.R. to John Pemberton . 7. 10
£ 7. 10

10, John McCalla Taylor
Dwelling . £30 . 18
£28. of Elizabeth Clifton . 16. 16
£ 34. 16
G.R. to Joseph Wharton 16. 5
to John Pemberton 7. 10 . 23. 15
£ 11. 1

John Bringhurst Merchant
1 Horse . 13. 4
£80. of Samuel Morton . 48
Land in Southwark . 1. 16
£6. of John Baley . 3. 12
£ 54. 1. 4
Annuity to Judah Foulke . 30
£ 24. 1. 4
Head & Estate £2. 11

4, John Oliver Captain
And for William Faulkner Estate
21, £12. of John Oliver . 7. 4
£23. of Jacob Shoemaker . 13. 16
£ 21

3, James Dickinson

Fig. 2. Assessment page of the Fifteenth Eighteen-Penny Provincial Tax, 13 March 1772, for the City and County of Philadelphia. Courtesy of The Historical Society of Pennsylvania.

The **fourth step** was to list tax defaulters, those individuals who had not, for one reason or another, paid the taxes due. When the tax collector arrived at the door, he sometimes found that the individual had moved to another county, was deceased, or over the taxable age limit for the poll tax. The collector would then make a list of tax defaulters and would sometimes enter an explanation for nonpayment: gone to Texas, dead, too old. In the example from Orange County, Virginia, 1738, in Fig. 3, there are several notations of "ran away," as well as "not found," and "a

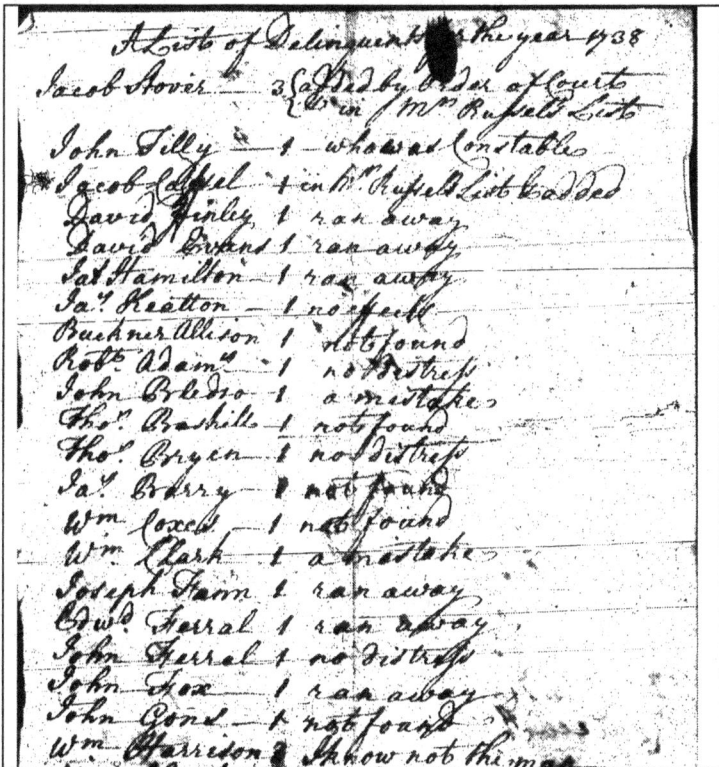

Fig. 3. Orange County, Virginia, Defaulters List, 1738. Courtesy of The Library of Virginia.

mistake." The last notation in this list states: "I know not the man."

Locating Tax Records

Even though taxes were collected every year, the records may be difficult or impossible to locate.

- Not all tax records have survived, especially in counties where the courthouse was destroyed or the records damaged by water or neglect.
- Not all tax records have been microfilmed. You may have to study them in the original ledger books in the local courthouse or an archive.
- Not all tax records for consecutive years are available, making it difficult to follow an individual year by year.

Your first job is to establish whether the tax records you need for your research exist. A state-by-state overview of existing tax records and their location is available in *Red Book: American State, County, & Town Sources,* edited by Alice Eichholz. This reference should be your first step in familiarizing yourself with the location in which your ancestors lived and the types and availability of tax records.

The most extensive microfilmed collection of tax records is in the Family History Library (FHL) in Salt Lake City. Begin your search in the Family History Catalog online at www.familysearch.org, select the "Library" tab, and then the "Family History Library Catalog" tab. Use the "Place" command and enter the county name (without the word "county") and the state. You can then access a list of record groups that have been microfilmed. Look down the list of record groups for "Taxation." The "Taxation" category may contain a variety of tax records for a number of different time periods. When you have located a microfilm for the period you are researching, you can rent it for a small fee through a local Family History Center.

Place: Texas, Smith
Notes: Smith County was created in 1846.
Topics: Texas, Smith – Bible records
Texas, Smith – Court records
Texas, Smith – Land and property
Texas, Smith – Probate records
Texas, Smith – Taxation
Texas, Smith – Vital Records

If there is no listing for "Taxation" for the county in the FHL catalog, your next step should be to check the state archives for the appropriate state. Use a search engine such as Google™ or Yahoo® to find the website for the state archives of that state. Many state archives have online catalogs and finding aids that will allow you to search their holdings for tax records.

If the information about tax records is not listed online, contact the state archive using the telephone number or e-mail address listed on the website to ask about available records. Confirm with archive personnel that the tax ledgers or microfilms of the records are available for research. Some state archives will allow you to borrow microfilmed records through InterLibrary Loan programs for a nominal fee. If the tax ledgers exist but have not been microfilmed, you may need to visit the archive in person or hire a researcher to examine the records for you.

If the tax records are not in the state archive, it is possible that they are still in the courthouse of the county you are researching. This is especially true of counties in the western United States. If the records are still in the care and control of the county courthouse, you will need to contact the county clerk to learn whether the courthouse will allow access to these records. When you have verified that the records are available for research, you can plan your visit to that courthouse or hire a local researcher who can make that visit for you. Even if you do not want to pay a researcher for extensive courthouse research, you may find that a local researcher can confirm that the records you are seeking exist and that they are available for study. Be as specific as you can in your request for tax records. All correspondence and requests should identify the county and time period.

Research Tax Records at Courthouse or Archive

If you decide to visit the state archive, the state library, or county courthouse in person, you can increase your productivity during the visit by being prepared.

- Learn as much as you can about the laws governing the state for the period you are researching. You can do this by reading books, journal articles, and Internet documents discussing law and taxation in the state.
- Contact the facility to confirm its schedule. Confirm opening and closing times, Saturday hours, and any upcoming holiday closures. Some small archives store records offsite and need time to retrieve them.
- Carry your most important data including surnames, places, and time spans with you. You will want to have the surnames of all the families you are researching in this

area as well as the names of all collateral relatives including sons-in-law, the maiden names of women who married into the family, and the names of neighbors and other close associates.

- Bring paper, pencils, and other travel supplies such as cash for photocopies, pencil sharpener, tissues, and note paper. It may be impossible to make photocopies of large tax ledgers, and you may find yourself sitting on the floor of a storeroom taking notes. Notebooks are usually restricted in research rooms although laptop computers may be allowed. You may also be able to use a digital camera although flash is usually restricted.

Consult Christine Rose's *Courthouse Research for Family Historians* for more information about successful record searches inside the local courthouse.

Tax Records as Substitutes for Census Records

Tax records are the best substitute for census records. The census taker came around once every ten years and often missed people. The tax collector came around every year and seldom missed anyone. For the period before 1790 when there were no censuses, tax records are a good source of information. They can also be a valuable replacement for the significant loss of early census records. Tax records for the period between 1880 and 1900 can be an important substitute for the 1890 census, most of which was destroyed in a fire.

Verify County Formation Date

Most real estate, personal property, and poll taxes were assessed and collected at the county level. Since tax records were maintained by the governmental agency that created them, you will find most of them at the county level. To determine where your ancestor was living at any particular time, it is important to know what county had jurisdiction at that time. Reference books such as *Red Book* and Everton's *Handybook for Genealogists: United States of America* list the dates of county formation as well as parent counties. Thorndale and Dollarhide's *Map Guide to the U.S. Federal Censuses, 1790-1920*, provides a pictorial view of county formation at ten-year intervals.

As America expanded, county boundaries changed frequently. In colonial times, for example, your ancestors living in the western part of Henrico County, Virginia, in 1727 would have found themselves in Goochland County in 1728, and the taxes would have then been collected in Goochland. In 1749 the western part of Goochland County became Cumberland County so the taxes were then collected in Cumberland. Records were not transferred when a new county was formed, so it is vital that you keep track of county formation dates even if your ancestors never actually moved. The records are always located in the county *as it existed at the time of the creation of the record.*

Exception: Original land tax records beginning in 1863 for those Virginia counties that are now part of West Virginia were turned over to the West Virginia Auditor's Office by order of an act passed by the Virginia General Assembly in February 1892. County records that were kept by the Virginia counties that became part of West Virginia remain under the original county name.

Following the Records Year By Year

The most valuable tax records are those that cover a period of consecutive years. If you are able to trace an individual through several years of tax records, you might see him progress from a landless young man who has reached the age of 21 to a landowner who is taxed on land and livestock, then to a mature man who is joined on the tax rolls by males with the same surname who have themselves reached the age of 21. You might also find a widow who is taxed on the land and livestock left behind after her husband's death or an executor who is paying the tax on an estate. These records can allow you to estimate birth and death dates and make hypotheses about the existence of deeds and even marriage records.

Isolated Records

Important discoveries can also be made on the basis of just a few tax records. The tax records of New York City for 1807, for example, list the owner and adult inhabitants of each dwelling. The owners were taxed on the land and structures as well as their personal property. The renters were taxed only on their personal property. This single tax list helps to establish the location and personal worth of New York City dwellers by first and last name in this early period.

In the example in Fig. 4, David Titus owned one of two houses located at No. 93 Greenwich Street. The house was valued at $3,500, and he paid $18.20 in tax on the house and $1.04 tax on his

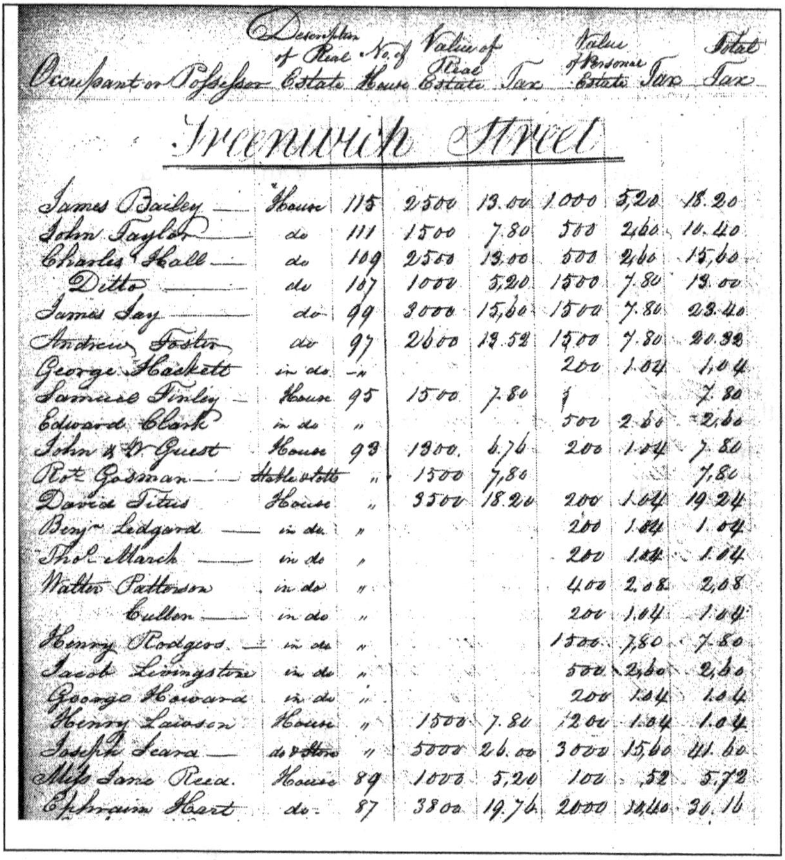

Occupant or Possessor	Description of Real Estate	No. of House	Value of Real Estate	Tax	Value of Personal Estate	Tax	Total Tax
Greenwich Street							
James Bailey	House	115	2500	13.00	1000	5.20	18.20
John Taylor	do	111	1500	7.80	500	2.60	10.40
Charles Hall	do	109	2500	13.00	500	2.60	15.60
Ditto	do	107	1000	5.20	1500	7.80	13.00
James Jay	do	99	3000	15.60	1500	7.80	23.40
Andrew Foster	do	97	2600	13.52	1500	7.80	20.32
George Hackett	in do	"			200	1.04	1.04
Samuel Finley	House	95	1500	7.80			7.80
Edward Clark	in do	"			500	2.60	2.60
John & W. Guest	House	93	1300	6.76	200	1.04	7.80
Robt Gosman	Stable & lotts	"	1500	7.80			7.80
David Titus	House	"	3500	18.20	200	1.04	19.24
Benjn Ledgard	in do	"			200	1.04	1.04
Thos March	in do	"			200	1.04	1.04
Walter Patterson	in do	"			400	2.08	2.08
Cullen	in do	"			200	1.04	1.04
Henry Rodgers	in do	"			1500	7.80	7.80
Jacob Livingston	in do	"			500	2.60	2.60
George Howard	in do	"			200	1.04	1.04
Henry Lawson	House	"	1500	7.80	200	1.04	1.04
Joseph Sears	do & Store	"	5000	26.00	3000	15.60	41.60
Miss Jane Reed	House	89	1000	5.20	100	.52	5.72
Ephraim Hart	do	87	3800	19.76	2000	10.40	30.16

Fig. 4. New York City Assessment Roll, 1807. Courtesy of Rosenthal Library, Queens College, Flushing, New York.

personal property. Renters included Benjamin Ledgard, Thomas March, Walter Patterson, Walter Cullin, Henry Rodgers, Jacob Livingston, and George Howard, who paid only the personal property tax. Note that Henry Rodgers owned $1,500 in personal property and paid $7.80 tax. Miss Jane Reed, a female, owned the house at No. 89 Greenwich Street, valued at $1,000, and $100 of personal property. Her tax bill was $5.72.

A single list of taxpayers for 1816 for Warren County, Ohio, makes it possible to identify land parcels in the county that were part of the Virginia Military District. Warren County straddled the boundary of the Virginia Military District, and some of the land in the county was divided into rectangular land parcels identified by range, township, and section number while others were identified by entry number in the Virginia Military District. You can use this information to search for records of landowners living in the Virginia Military District to determine whether they received bounty land for service in the Revolutionary War or purchased a land warrant from a veteran or his heirs.

Indexes: Never the Final Answer

Researchers who have never looked at the actual tax rolls may be asking: Isn't there an easier way? There are published indexes for some tax records, but, if you rely on indexes alone, you will miss several benefits of tax research. Published tax indexes typically list the names of taxpayers alphabetically and omit any indication of relationships, taxable items, and amount of tax collected. Even your ability to locate an ancestor in a specific county may be difficult when there are, for example, ten Applegate males listed in a single tax list for Westmoreland County, Pennsylvania. You will need to study specific tax information to distinguish between men with the same surname.

William H. Dumont, the editor of *Tax Lists, Westmoreland County, Pennsylvania, 1786-1810*, stated in his text that "the amount of taxes paid may be interesting but adds nothing of a genealogical nature."[1] Nothing could be further from the truth. The actual tax lists for Westmoreland County, Pennsylvania, included the amount of tax, the number of acres of land, value of the land and livestock. This Pennsylvania tax list also indicated "single man" status, information that can be very helpful in sorting out those Applegate males. Indexes are useful as a quick guide to determine whether your ancestor is included in the record, but you need to study the original tax records to verify the identity and location of your family members and gather more personal information.

A Word About Slaves

Historic tax laws, tax assessment and collection records include many references to "slaves," "black polls," "Negroes," and "free persons of color." These are the terms used in the original records, and they will be used throughout this book.

References to slaves enumerated with livestock and other personal property are true to the historical record and perhaps can be helpful to researchers. A few tax records give the first names of slaves and these scattered references could be useful in tracing slave ancestors who were bequeathed to family members, mentioned in deeds of gift, or granted manumission. Tax records also include the first and last name of free persons of color who were taxed in pre-Civil War records. In the post-Civil War period former slaves were added to the tax rolls for head taxes or personal property taxes. These records may provide important clues in identifying new heads of households as they assumed surnames and may help you link these surnames to former slaves enumerated in the 1870 U.S. census. In Georgia tax records of the post-war period, for example, you will find the names of freedmen listed under the name of an employer who paid their wages.

Finding the Right Record in the Wrong Place

Genealogists are always thrilled to locate the one record that unlocks the mystery they have been working hard to solve. Sometimes the answer appears in an unlikely place. This is certainly true of tax records. Information about taxes may appear in court records, auditor's records, deed books, immigration records, newspapers, and personal papers. Learning how to interpret tax records will help you recognize valuable information when it appears in an unlikely place. Caswell County, North Carolina, Will Book B, for example, includes a list of tax insolvents for the Nash and St. James Districts for 1787. Insolvent lists for the other six districts of Caswell County are not included.

Ready to Begin?

Tax records offer a great deal of research potential for genealogists. While there are some difficulties ahead, the lure of primary information about your ancestors should be irresistible to any researcher. Is it worth the effort? Absolutely. You wouldn't attempt to do basic genealogical research without the census records, and you won't want to pass up the valuable information waiting to be discovered in the tax records.

---

[1] William H. Dumont, editor, *Tax Lists, Westmoreland County, Pennsylvania, 1786-1810* (Washington, D.C.: National Genealogical Society, 1968), 4.

Chapter 2. Research Techniques

. . . the day may come when historians will realize that tax records tell the real story behind civilized life. How people were taxed, who was taxed, and what was taxed tell more about a society than anything else.

Charles Adams,
For Good and Evil: The Impact of Taxes on the Course of Civilization

Tax records contain information about your ancestor: his land and its location, other possessions, and perhaps even family relationships. This information will enable you to make hypotheses about your ancestor's life and lead you to other records. There are a number of research techniques that can be used to extract this information. Because of the variety of taxes and the frequency with which they were collected, most researchers should be able to find their ancestors in these records.

Types of Taxes

It is useful to start with some definitions of the various taxes that were collected.

poll tax: a flat tax levied on each taxable individual such as white males of taxable age, indentured servants, and slaves. This tax is also called a head tax or capitation tax. In colonial Virginia it was called a tithable tax.

land tax: a tax imposed on real estate owned, based on amount of land, its location, and sometimes its quality.

personal property tax: a tax levied on tangible property other than real estate such as vehicles, livestock, musical instruments, furniture, and jewelry.

Tax Records May Be Combined

Counties frequently combined the poll or head tax with personal property tax records, land tax records, or both. Some counties kept separate records for special tax levies, while some merely added additional columns to the forms already in use. Tax forms often reported how the tax funds were allocated between the town, county, and state, or for special taxes. From this information you can make inferences about the society in which your ancestor lived. Information collected about the number of children ages 6-18, for example, probably indicates that taxes were being allocated to publicly funded schools. Funds allocated to the poor farm or the insane asylum indicates the presence of these institutions.

A combined list for Salem, Massachusetts, for 1773 indicates that taxes were being collected for the province, the town, and the county. The town tax portion was twice that of the province and the county indicating that the town unit in Massachusetts supplied the majority of the governance.

How to Approach a Tax Record

Determine the year and specific county that you want to research. After you have examined available census records to identify your ancestor's location at both ends of the ten-year census interval, you can start your research in the appropriate county or counties. If there were two counties involved, examining tax records can help determine when he relocated from one place to the other. Of course, if the second county was formed from the first during the ten-year period between censuses, he might not have moved at all.

Examining tax records can also narrow the interval during which an immigrant arrived in the United States. Once you have found the earliest census in which he appears, work backwards through the tax records for that county. Remember that individuals are usually listed in the tax rolls one year after their arrival in the county.

Start by examining the tax record for a single year. Are the lists identified by the name of the tax collector, by a numbered tax district, by township and range, by militia district, or by school district? Does this information help you narrow your search to the part of the county where your ancestor lived?

Look at the column headings. Are they printed on the form or are they handwritten? Are the column headings omitted or illegible? Do you understand what the headings stand for? For example, is the government taxing acres of land, cattle, horses, carriages and wagons? Are there columns for white and black polls? Is this a land tax record only or a personal property tax or poll tax list that includes almost everyone? Or does the list combine different kinds of taxes?

You should now read the entire tax list for the county for one year as you search for your ancestor, collaterals, in-laws, and known associates. Studying the entire list will help to familiarize yourself with spelling variations, handwriting style, and list organization. Did you find the name of the ancestor you were looking for?

If the answer is yes, congratulations! Write down the tax district designation, and the source of the tax list (microfilm number, original ledger), and the tax information you found. You may want to create a chart or spreadsheet to record the information. Then look at the tax record for the next year. You may discover that your ancestor stayed in the same district with the same neighbors over an extended period of time. Or you may discover that at some point the entire tax district disappeared! Check county formation dates to learn whether that part of the old county became part of a new county. In 1858, for example, Land District 13 of Fayette County, Georgia, disappeared from the tax records of that county and was added to the tax records of newly created Clayton County.

Sometimes a taxpayer was listed under another person's name. If a neighbor was acting as your ancestor's agent, for example, your ancestor's name might be listed under the neighbor's name. Extended families frequently lived in close proximity to one another, and their information will often be in the same tax records as your ancestor. Identifying kinship groups can also be a way of distinguishing individuals with the same name. Studying the records of collateral relatives may also help identify a married daughter. Consequently, you will want to study tax records for your ancestor's relatives, neighbors, and associates.

If you were unsuccessful in locating your ancestor on the first try, recheck your original information. Perhaps you were off by a year or two. Skip ahead a year or two and read through the next list. It is possible that a single man living away from his usual neighborhood, perhaps working as a hired hand, could have been missed by the tax collector. Once that man married and lived in his own dwelling, he should appear in the records. When you have located your ancestor in a tax record, work backward to determine when he was first added to the tax list.

Identify Information Being Collected

It is imperative that you learn what information was recorded in each column of the tax record. If the column headings are missing or unclear, you will have to look for an explanation elsewhere, perhaps in a state guide to tax records, in a journal article about tax records, or in the state tax codes. The order of the columns may also change from one year to the next as information being collected changed. Georgia county tax forms for 1858, for example, listed the number of children in a family between the ages of 8 and 18. In 1861 the forms listed the number of children in a family between the ages of 6 and 18. In some records cattle may be taxed one year and become exempt the next. Stud horses may be listed in a separate column because they represented a source of income and were usually valued at a higher rate.

The tax rate could also change from year to year. The lowest total tax charged on a single man with no land and no personal property will be a poll tax. Personal property taxes on livestock, carriages, and other possessions may be the result of assessment of the value of an item or may be levied at a flat rate. Land taxes may be based on the quality of the land being taxed. It is common to see columns headed "1st," "2nd," and "3rd" indicating first, second, and third quality land. Georgia added a fourth quality, "pine." You can determine the tax rate for a single category of land by dividing the tax charged by the number of acres. If there were 100 acres of first quality land and the tax was $5.00, the tax was five cents per acre.

Sources for Interpreting Tax Information

Record repositories may be able to provide information about the tax records they hold. The National Archives publishes indexes, preliminary indexes, and special lists for its major record collections. These finding aids contain an introduction describing the history and functions of the agency that created the records as well as a description of the records themselves. Frequently, individual states publish pamphlets and finding aids describing the records and their contents. These may be either online or in print. The Library of Virginia, for example, has posted online tutorials on its website describing tithables, land tax records, and personal property tax records for the state. The Philadelphia Office of the City Commissioners has posted a "Philadelphia Information Locator Service Archival Record Series" online that describes in detail the city's archival holdings. These holdings include several early tax records for the colony and later the state of Pennsylvania.

Consider Spelling Variations

New researchers sometimes have trouble recognizing that their surname was spelled in a wide variety of ways. There was absolutely no consistency in the way any one individual would spell his own name, much less agreement among census takers and tax collectors about the "right" way to spell a surname. The name may even be spelled differently within the same document. Thus, you may find "Askew," "Askque," "Askq," "Asku," "Ayscue," "Askyou," or "Ascough" in the tax rolls for one year and a different spelling for the same individual the next year. You will need to use all the clues in a record to determine whether this is indeed your ancestor.

The problem is even trickier for names that were unfamiliar to English-speaking authorities. The French surname "Reynau" may have been spelled "Reno" and the German surname "Oachs" written as "Oaks."

Tax lists were usually alphabetized by the first letter of the taxpayer's surname. Start by looking for your ancestor under the appropriate letter. If you don't find him, he may still be in the tax list under another letter. For example, prefixes such as "Mc" may be missing or written merely as an initial "M." Some prefixes were written as middle names rather than as part of the surname. If you don't find your Fitzgerald ancestor under "F," look under "G." You may find him there as "Gerrall." The same is true of any names with the prefix "von," or "van."

Become Familiar With Notations and Abbreviations

Sometimes the most challenging part of studying old records is deciphering the handwriting and the notation style used by a particular recorder. Fortunately, when you are looking at a list of names, the surname you are researching often seems to jump out at you. Take a few minutes to look at the entire list and learn to recognize the way the recorder wrote capital letters and numbers. The capital letters "L" and "S" may look similar but are easy to distinguish in an alphabetized list. The use of a figure that appears as "fs" stands for a double s. The name that appears to be written as "Mofs," for example, is probably "Moss." You will also want to become familiar with the style of writing used for numbers. The number "8," for example, is often written as "σ" or "δ" while the number "1" may resemble the number "7." Consult a book such as Kip Sperry's *Reading Early American Handwriting* to familiarize yourself with common handwriting forms. It will make your task easier and your search more successful.

Abbreviations were common in tax documents and may include "Do" for "ditto" or "the same" and "anc" for "ancient," meaning too old to pay the poll tax. Other notations may include "agt" for "agent," who might be paying the taxes for someone else; "dec'd" for "deceased"; and "exr" for "executor."

Tax collectors frequently used nicknames, occupations, and relationships to identify and differentiate between men of the same surname. You will frequently find a notation such as "John Cook, Patroller" or "Martin Smith, son of Mitchell." You also need to be aware of the colonial custom of referring to individuals with the same name in a single community as "senior" and "junior" according to their ages. This is not proof that they were related. It was merely a method used by the courts and the tax collectors to indicate that they were separate individuals. When the older individual died, the junior individual might become the senior if there were still younger men with the same name in the community. This explains the appearance of Shem Cook, Senior, in the records of Granville County, North Carolina, several years after the death of one Shem Cook, Senior.

Research Example: Separate Men with the Same Name in the Same County

For genealogical researchers faced with two or more individuals with the same name in the same county, land tax records that place one individual in one tax district and another individual in another district can help distinguish between the two. While it is certainly possible that one individual could own all the land taxed under a single surname, it is less likely that two individuals living in different parts of the same county are the same individual. Traveling across the county to tend fields or monitor livestock would have been time consuming before the early 1900s.

A North Carolina list of taxable property for 1815 includes three individuals with similar names: John Stone, John B. Stone, and Jonathan Stone. From the information in the tax records, we can hypothesize that John Stone, owner of 292 acres of land, who was taxed on ten adult slaves and no white polls, was a mature male older than the taxable age limit of 50. We can further hypothesize

Table 1. Stone Family Tax Record, North Carolina, 1815

Name	No. of Acres	Value Per Acre ($)	Total Land Value ($)	No. of White Polls	No. of Black Polls
Stone, John	292	4	1,170	0	10
Stone, John B.	0	0	0	1	1
Stone, Jonathan	245	4	980	1	4

that John B. Stone, a man who owned no land and was liable for one white poll and one black poll, was a young man who had a personal slave but did not yet own land in his own right. Jonathan Stone, a man who owned 245 acres of land, four adult slaves, and owed one white poll tax, might be a man in his middle years, younger than 50, who owned both land and slaves. Further research verifies some of these assumptions and disproves others:

- John Stone, a veteran of the Revolutionary War, was born on 26 February 1760[2] according to his pension application and was therefore 55 years old in 1815.

- John B. Stone was identified as the son of John Stone in his father's Revolutionary War pension application. According to the application, the son was born in 1793, making him 22 years old in 1815.[3]

- Jonathan Stone, also a veteran of the Revolutionary War, was born between 1750 and 1760,[4] making him 55 to 65 years old in 1815. Since he was above the age limit to be taxed on his own poll,[5] the white poll may be a son who was over the age of 21 or a white servant of taxable age.

The Revolutionary War pension application of John Stone also indicates that John Stone and Jonathan Stone were, in fact, brothers,[6] something that modern Americans would not readily guess because they would assume these names were variations of the same name.

Doing the Math

Indexes to tax lists frequently omit all information about the number of acres being taxed, the number of polls being taxed, value of land, and even the total amount of tax collected. It would be easy to ignore the numerical information altogether if all you want to do is locate your ancestor. The amounts, however, can provide valuable clues for the genealogist who wants to understand the economic position of his ancestor (rich or poor, landowner, slaveholder) and how that compares to the economic situation of the local community. To get this information, you may have to calculate the amount of tax being charged for each taxable item, and it may seem a bit challenging.

Table 2. Tennessee Tax List, 1833

Head of Household	No. of Acres	White Polls	Black Polls	Other Taxable Items	Total Tax Due
Bostick, A.	0	1	2	1C2W*	7.00
Chaffin, Ward	200	0	0	1 stove	7.00
Dale, E.W.	432	1	7	1C4W	20.07
Frierson, Gardner	0	1	2		2.00
Gante, J.P.	0	1	0		.50
George, Willie	0	1	1		1.25
Groves, John B.	0	1	2	1 stove	7.00

*1 carriage, 2 wheels

Research Example: Estimate Wealth of An Ancestor

Let's look at a tax list for Tennessee for 1833 extracted in Table 2. Start with the simplest entry, J.P. Gante, who was charged 50 cents for one white poll (himself). Willie George was charged $1.25 in taxes—50 cents for his own white poll and 75 cents for his one black poll. Using these figures, you can calculate that Gardner Frierson was charged 50 cents for his one white poll, and 75 cents each for two black polls. John B. Groves paid the same $2 in taxes for his one white poll and two black polls—plus $5 in tax for the stove. By using these amounts for the white and black polls, you can calculate that land was taxed at one penny per acre because Ward Chaffin paid $5 tax on the stove plus $2 for 200 acres of land. That makes it easy to calculate that A. Bostick paid an additional $5 in tax for his one carriage with two wheels (1C2W) while E.W. Dale paid an additional $10 in tax for his carriage with four wheels. Taxpayers who pay a relatively high tax bill can certainly be assumed to be financially well off, although it was possible to lose everything in the next depression.

Table 3 includes a portion of the Fayette County, Georgia tax list for 1828. This record listed the number of slaves, number of acres, quality of land, lot and district number, and total tax amount due. Even though there is no column for white polls, single white males such as Kindred Blackstock and Joseph Chapman who owned no personal property or real estate were charged a poll tax of 15 cents. The tax on slaves was 12.5 cents per slave. Leonard Davis was apparently over the age required for payment of a white poll but paid the 12.5 cents for his single slave. Adkison, who owned 202½ acres (standard Georgia lot size) of third quality land, was charged 31 cents tax. Black, who owned 101¼ acres of second quality land (better quality, half the amount) was also charged 31 cents tax. By subtracting 15 cents for their personal poll tax, it appears that the total land tax for each was 16 cents. You should also notice that there is a column listing the county

Table 3. Georgia Tax Digest, Fayette County, 1828

Head of Household	No. of Slaves	Acres of 1st Quality Land	Acres of 2nd Quality Land	Acres of 3rd Quality Land	Lot No.	District No.	County Where Land Is	Tax Due
Adkison, William				202½	41	9	Fayette	.31
Blackstock, Kindred								.15
Black, Samuel			101¼		181	9	Fayette	.31
Christian, William	1			40	419	21	Paulding	.43
Chapman, Joseph								.15
Davis, Leonard	1							.125

location of the land being taxed. When you are studying tax records, it is important to know what the law was at any given time. In Georgia before 1847, for example, land taxes were paid in the county where the owner lived, not where the land was located.

Records that Report Only Assessed Value

You will sometimes find records that report the assessed value of the property without specifying the tax collected. These are wonderful sources of information about the possessions and dwellings of residents. The provincial tax collected in Pennsylvania in the 1770s, for example, is a detailed list of the assessed value of taxable property. Records were headed with location and assessor's name and list property owners, their occupation or status (such as widow), valuation of each category of property, and the total value of their holdings. Dwellings were assessed at 60 percent of their value and slaves at a flat £4 each. Amounts collected as rents or interest on debts were included as income, and amounts paid out to support certain dependents were deducted from the total assessed value.

Table 4. Pennsylvania Provincial Tax,
Philadelphia City and County, 1772

	Assessed Value		
	Pounds	Shillings	Pence
Levi Marks, Taylor			
Negro	4		
7 acres Land	6		
£12 of Mary McNamara	7	4	-
Total Assessment £	17	4	
Thomas Douglas	-	-	-
Joanna Anthony, Widow			
Dwelling, £40	24		
£35 of Thomas Douglas	21		
£20 of John Keen	12		
£6 of Adam Fox	3	12	
GR of Joseph Moore	6	10	
1 Negro	4		
Total Assessment £	71	2	
Thomas Bond Junr., Merchant			
Dwelling, £50	30		
1 Negro	4		
1 Horse		13	4
£50 of Levi Marks	30	-	-
Subtotal £	64	13	4
GR to Deborah Norris, £6			
GR to Rebecca Venables, £11	17		
Total Assessment £	47	13	4

£1 = 20 shillings
GR of = grant received from an individual
GR to = grant paid to an individual

In Table 4, which shows a portion of the Pennsylvania Provincial Tax of 1772 for Philadelphia, Joanna Anthony, a widow, is listed as the owner of a house valued at £40. The assessed value was 60 percent of £40 or £24. She apparently collected rents—assessed at 60 percent—from Thomas Douglas, John Keen, and Adam Fox. She received money from Joseph Moore, perhaps interest on a debt, and owned one Negro, for whom she was assessed £4. The total assessed value of her property was £71, 2 shillings. Her tax bill would have been a fraction of the total assessed value.

Paying Taxes in the Coin of the Realm

The American colonies were chronically short of hard currency. British pounds sterling were almost nonexistent in the colonies. Spanish silver dollars and French coins were more common but were quickly exported to England as payment for imports. Colonists turned to alternative means of payment including barter, commodities, and private promissory notes. Colonial legislatures passed laws specifying the official rate of exchange for local crops such as cereal grains, corn, tobacco, and rice when they were used to pay taxes. Other lawful commodities used in place of hard currency included beaver skins, cattle, and wampum (strings of beads made from shells).[7]

The use of commodities in payment for taxes presented significant problems because commodities had to be delivered, inspected, valued, stored, preserved, and then sold or distributed as payment for various government projects. North Carolina passed its first tax in order to fund the building of a courthouse in every district. The North Carolina Assembly then had to levy a second tax to finance the construction of warehouses in every district to store the commodities received in payment of taxes.[8] Colonists quickly learned to reduce their tax burden by shipping the worst products to colonial treasuries while selling their better commodities on the open market.

The Massachusetts Bay Colony issued the first paper money in the American colonies in 1690 to pay colonial troops and other expenses resulting from an inter-colonial war between the possessions of France and England.[9] By 1712, seven more colonies had issued paper currency.[10] Each colony issued its own currency, usually called bills of credit or "current money," which could be used to pay all obligations including taxes. Colonies also periodically issued new currency in an effort to foil counterfeiters.

Calculating With Pounds, Shillings, and Pence

From the earliest colonial days into the 1800s, public tax records were calculated in pounds, shillings, and pence. The value of Spanish dollars and French coins as well as commodities and printed colonial bills of credit were tied to the value of British currency.

Throughout the colonial period, the British pound (£) equaled 20 shillings, and one shilling equaled 12 pence. Therefore, one pound equaled 240 pence. When you add a column of numbers, the amounts would look like this:

```
    2.14.6 (2 pounds, 14 shillings, 6 pence)
  + 3.09.8 (3 pounds, 9 shillings, 8 pence)

    5.23.14 = 5.24.2 = 6.4.2 (6 pounds, 4 shillings, 2 pence
```

The total is 5 pounds, 23 shillings, and 14 pence. The 14 pence equals 1 shilling, 2 pence, and the resulting 24 shillings, 2 pence equals 1 pound, 4 shillings, 2 pence. Add the 1 pound to the original 5 pounds for a total of 6 pounds, 4 shillings, 2 pence.

Research Example: Estimate Wealth of an Ancestor

Whether the tax was collected in British pounds or dollars, you can determine your ancestor's financial position by comparing his tax bill to that of others in his community. Let's look at an example from a Massachusetts tax list for 1773. The tax amounts were recorded in pounds, shillings, and pence.

Table 5. Massachusetts Town Tax Collection, 1773
£1= 20 shillings, 1 shilling = 12 pence

Head of Household	Polls	For Houses and Lands	For Personal Estate and Income by Trade	Sum Total of Tax
Stephen Abbot	0.5.1	0.4.6	0.4.6	0.14.1
George Abbot	0.5.1	0.18.0	1.0.6	2.3.7
Nathl Atkins	0.10.2	0.9.0	3.9.0	1.3.0
Saml Barton for self & mother	0.10.2	3.18.0	2.1.3	6.9.5
Sarah Adams	0	0.7.6	0.2.6	0.0.10

The lowest tax charged was 5 shillings, 1 pence (0.5.1) apparently for one adult male. Stephen and George Abbot each paid that amount for his poll, while George Abbot paid additional taxes for his house, lands, personal property, and income from trade. Apparently, George Abbot was the older and wealthier of the two

Abbot men. Nathaniel Atkins, who paid a total of 10 shillings, 2 pence in poll taxes, apparently was paying for two adult males (0.5.1 x 2). Samuel Barton, who was paying for himself and his mother, is also paying for two adult males (perhaps his son or a brother). Neither his mother nor Sarah Adams, a widow, would have been charged a poll tax.

Forming a Hypothesis

After you have studied tax records for an ancestor, you should be ready to form a hypothesis about his financial situation based on his tax status. Such a hypothesis might read like this:

> *John Smith was a relatively wealthy man in the years between 1850 and 1860 because he owned 200 acres of land and 20 slaves between the taxable ages of 12 and 50, according to the county tax records. If the average value of each adult slave were $500, he possessed personal property worth approximately $10,000 and real estate valued at $1,000.*

Given this hypothesis regarding John Smith, your research plan might look like this:

1. Check the census records for 1850 and 1860. The 1850 census lists the value of any real estate owned. The 1860 census lists the value of both real estate and personal property, which would include the value of any slaves owned.

2. Review the U.S. Census Slave Schedules for 1850 and 1860 to check the ages of John Smith's slaves.

3. Search for land records in this county for John Smith to determine his real estate holdings.

4. Determine his age and the extent of his family from the 1850 and 1860 U.S. Census Population Schedules.
5. Search the U.S. Census Agricultural Schedules for 1850 and 1860 for the number of acres cultivated, crops, and other agricultural products (milk, butter, cheese, butchered meat).

Another hypothesis for another ancestor might read:

> *William Jones was a poor man in the years between 1870 and 1880 because he was not taxed on any land during those years. According to the tax records, his only personal property was one cow and one mule.*

To continue research on William Jones, you might take the following actions:

1. Check the census records for 1860 and 1870. These censuses list the value of both real estate and personal property.
2. Search the personal property tax lists for Jones for several years to determine whether his property had increased or decreased.
3. If Jones owned land before 1870, based on the 1860 U.S. census, check for the sale of land for failure to pay taxes. Such delinquent land tax sales were frequent in the defeated Confederate states between 1865 and 1875.
4. Check court records for homestead exemption requests. Several states passed such laws to provide a minimum level of protection against the seizure of homes and

personal property. Often the exemption reduced the amount of property tax due on a primary residence.

Summary of Research Techniques

To successfully research a tax record:

- Search for tax records, usually at the county level, for the correct time period.
- Learn what the column headings are in all tax records to determine what information was being collected.
- Consider the many spelling variations for the surnames of your ancestors.

After you have located an ancestor in the tax records:

- Do a year-by-year comparison of tax records, if available.
- Calculate the amount of tax.
- Look for collateral relatives in the same tax records.
- Write a formal hypothesis.
- Develop a preliminary research plan.

As you study tax records you will need to develop specific skills to decipher old handwriting, recognize common abbreviations, and calculate tax amounts in pounds, shillings, and pence to enhance your understanding of the information presented.

---

[2] John Stone Revolutionary War Pension Application, File W19403, Revolutionary War Pension and Bounty-Land Warrant Application Files, M805, (Washington, D.C.: National Archives), Roll 777.

[3] John Stone Revolutionary War Pension Application, File W19403. A handwritten family Bible page in the file lists the birth date of John B. Stone and names him as a child of John Stone.

[4] Jonathan Stone household, 1830 U.S. census, Franklin County, North Carolina, Edwards District, page 342, line 7, National Archives micropublication M19, roll 120, includes one adult male in the 70-80 year old category. The same census also lists the John Stone household, 1830 U.S. census, Franklin County, North Carolina, Edwards District, page 342, line 12, National Archives micropublication M19, roll 120, with one adult male in the 70-80 year old category.

5 Raymond A. Winslow, Jr., "Chapter 14: Tax and Fiscal Records," *North Carolina Research, Genealogy and Local History*, Helen Leary, editor (Raleigh, North Carolina: North Carolina Genealogical Society, 1996), 232. A North Carolina law in 1801 exempted free white males over the age of 50 from the poll tax.

6 John Stone Revolutionary War Pension Application, File W19403, M805, (Washington, D.C.: National Archives), Roll 777, identified Jonathan Stone as the brother of John Stone.

7 Alvin Rabushka, "The Colonial Roots of American Taxation, 1607-1700," *Policy Review*, No. 114, August-September 2002, 65.

8 Paul M. McCain, *The County Court in North Carolina Before 1750* (Durham, North Carolina: Duke University Press, 1954), 109.

9 Charles H.J. Douglas, *The Financial History of Massachusetts From the Organization of the Massachusetts Bay Company to the American Revolution*, Studies in History, Economics and Public Law, Vol. 1, No. 4 (New York: AMS Press, 1892), 64.

10 Rabushka, "The Colonial Roots of American Taxation, 1607-1700," 66.

Chapter 3. Poll Taxes

How much better to have been slain than to go about with a tax on our heads!

Boadicea, leader of native Britons
opposing the invading Roman army, 60 A.D.

Taxpayers throughout history may have shared Boadicea's dire preference but, for the most part, they have paid their taxes in a fairly orderly fashion, and governments have recorded their payments. That is a boon for genealogical researchers. Tax records—especially head tax records that enumerate most adult males in the community—help us locate ancestors in a precise area at times when census records are not available. U.S. census records start with the 1790 census, but Virginia, Delaware, Kentucky, New Jersey, Tennessee, and Georgia census records for 1790 have been lost. The 1800 census records for many of the counties in these states were also lost. Tax records can be important substitutes for these missing census records.

The word "poll" means "head," and poll taxes were taxes paid for each head that was taxable. Tax records based on heads or polls exist for various times and locations throughout American history, and they are worth locating. They can serve as a census for a location and can verify the presence of an individual in a particular year and place. A consecutive series of poll tax records can establish the length of residence of an individual in a particular location, document the growth of families as young men came of age and were added to the tax rolls in their own right, indicate an individual's removal from that location, or the death of the taxpayer. Head or poll tax records, even when they exist merely as lists of names in a specific county, can help narrow your search for other kinds of records.

Taxes "By the Poll" Were Earliest American Taxes

Poll taxes were collected in most of the American colonies as a simplified means of funding the relatively modest financial needs of the government. In the earliest colonial period, poll taxes were levied on a one-time basis for a specific purpose, such as building a courthouse in the county or a bridge over a large stream. They soon became part of the established tax structure.

Poll tax laws were often the first tax laws passed in a new territory because no assessment of value was required. Therefore, this type of tax was the easiest to calculate and collect. The Ohio poll tax law of 1800 is typical:

> *Sec. 1: That all able bodied free male inhabitants of the age of twenty-one years and upwards, who shall be found resident in any county in this territory, on the first day of May in every year, he and they are hereby declared subject to a poll tax in the county in which they shall be found resident on said day. . . . Provided that such poll-tax shall not exceed fifty cents upon each person subject thereto, in one year, to be levied and collected by the same persons and in the same manner, as other*

*county rates and levies are and shall be levied and
collected . . . .*

*Sec. 3: It shall be the duty of each head of a family,
when called upon by the [tax commissioner] to
give in the number and names of free male
inhabitants of the age of twenty-one years and
upwards, resident. . . on the first day of May.* [11]

Another example is the Arizona territorial poll tax for 1874. A poll
tax of three dollars was levied on each male 21 years of age and
over. Fifty percent of the amount collected went to support the
county and 50 percent went to support the territorial
government.[12]

Massachusetts Poll Tax, 1646

The General Court of the Massachusetts Bay Colony approved
taxation on general property in 1634 "to defray publique
charges."[13] In 1646 a poll tax rate of 2.5 shillings per poll was
levied on each adult male 16 years of age and over. This was in
addition to a property tax of a penny per pound tax on the value
of all personal property and real estate as well as a faculty tax on
the income and gains of artisans and skilled laborers.

The poll tax was a flat tax, but the General Court had the power to
double or even triple the rate. Since the tax was the same for each
individual no matter how rich or poor, the poll tax created a
greater tax burden on the poorer classes. Each year the three units
of government in the Massachusetts Bay Colony—the province,
the county, and the town—drew up a list of proposed
expenditures. They then determined the amount of tax money

required and applied a rate or multiplier of tax designed to generate the required funds.[14] For example, the basic poll tax rate was set at 1 shilling, 8 pence per poll in 1653 but levied at 26 rates (1 shilling, 8 pence x 26) to pay for King Philip's War (1675-1676) and 37 rates (1 shilling, 8 pence x 37) in 1689-1690 for a war against the French and eastern Indian tribes.[15]

Virginia Tithables

In March 1624 the Virginia General Assembly mandated a head tax of ten pounds of tobacco "upon every male head above sixteen years of age now living (not including such as arrived since the beginning of July last)."[16] Then in 1629 Virginia established a tithable system based on the head tax for the support of the civil government.

The General Assembly defined tithables as white males aged 16 and over and required that "every master of a family, and every freeman is to pay five pounds of tobacco per poll . . . for the defraying of publique charges."[17] In the 1640s, the Assembly defined taxpayers as masters of families who were "responsible for all public duties, tithes and charges due from all persons in their families."[18] By 1705, the Assembly had consolidated various legal definitions of tithables as all free white adult males age 16 and over, as well as white male indentured servants age 14 and over, white female indentured servants age 16 and over, male slaves aged 12 and over, and all Negro, mulatto, and Indian women age 16 years and over.[19] In tithable lists, which were written by the taxpayer himself, the head of the household was listed first, followed by his sons or nephews of the same surname, his white indentured servants, and finally the slaves who were listed by first name only. Table 6 provides an example of this type of list.

Table 6. Tithable List, Surry County, Virginia, 8 June 1699

List of Tithables	No. of Tithables
Benj. Harrison Esq., John Simonds, Robin, Harry, Dick, Tom, Samboe, Jack, Mingo, Will, George, Cato, Mary, Betty, Great Jone, Frank, Little Jone	17
Patrick Lashley, Walter Lashley	2
Fardinando Jarrett, 1 negroe Frank	2
Thos. Bage, Jno. Partridge & Jemmy an Indian	3
Mr. Thos. Flood, Jno Avery & Jno. Glover	3

Because the tithable or taxable age for white males was 16 years of age, it is possible to estimate the birth date of an individual who is added to an established family group by subtracting 16 from the tax year in which he first appears. White males were expected to remain on the tax rolls until old age, generally age 50. At that

> *To the Worshipful Gentlemen of the County Court of Orange County the humble Petition of Matthew Blanckenbücher humbly sheweth that your humble Petitioner is fifty two years of age as the testimonial letter of his birthday from Germany shew, & that he always being sick is not able to do any work, & that in this condition he was for these three years. Therefore your petitioner humbly requests that your Worships would please to clear him to pay any Levys further and your Petitioner shall be bound forever to pray.*
>
> *Orange County, 1746 21 May   Matthew Blanckenbücher*

Fig. 5. Petition of Matthew Blanckenbücher to the Court of Orange County, Virginia, to be excused from paying taxes.

point, they were not charged a tithable for themselves although they were still liable for the tithables in their household.

The courts were responsible for settling questions of age. Slaves were frequently presented to the court, which would determine their ages for the record. The courts also had the power to excuse individuals from paying taxes based on their age, poverty, or disability. Matthew Blanckenbücker presented his petition (Fig. 5) to the Orange County, Virginia, court in 1746 along with evidence that he was past the age of 50.

The Tithable Process

Starting in 1663, each head of household in Virginia was required to submit a list of his tithables naming each tithable who was taxable. These lists were due on June 10; age was determined as of June 9.

Upon receiving the individual tithable lists, the tax collector would organize them into roughly alphabetical order by first letter of the surname and post the lists for public inspection. Severe penalties were imposed for concealing tithables by omitting them from the list or by sending older sons out of the county during tax time. If a citizen noted a discrepancy in the list, he could report it to the tax collector. If his tip were upheld, he was entitled to a reward—1,000 pounds of tobacco or a slave forfeited by the errant list-maker.[20]

A standard feature of most tithable lists was the Defaulters' List. This list of people who had failed to pay their tithables usually appeared at the end of each parish list or at the back of the tax record book for that year. Because tithable lists were submitted several months in advance of the collection of the tax, the taxpayer might have moved to a different district or county by the time the tax collector came around to collect the tax. For example, Shem Cook was recorded as a tax defaulter in 1756 with three tithables in Orange County, Virginia.[21] However, deed records indicate that he had purchased land in Amelia County, Virginia, in February, 1756 and paid for his three tithables there.

Poll Books and Voting Rights

Elections for members of the Virginia House of Burgesses during the 17th and 18th centuries were conducted publicly. Candidates appeared at the polling location, and each man who was qualified to cast his vote based on his age and property ownership announced his vote. The amount of land necessary to qualify a voter differed for town and rural residents, town land being considered more valuable than rural land.

The sheriff recorded the votes in ledgers called poll books. According to the Library of Virginia, which holds a few surviving poll books in its collection, "The presence of a name on a Poll Book should in most instances be adequate proof that the person owned the requisite number of acres of land in the county. . . .[however,] the presence of a name on a poll list does not prove that a person lived in the county because men were legally able to vote in any jurisdiction in which they owned land."[22]

After the American Revolution some states used the payment of the poll or head tax as a substitute for land ownership as a requirement for voting, which broadened voting eligibility. New Hampshire, Delaware, Georgia, and North Carolina adopted state constitutions allowing men to vote if they paid any state tax, and each of these states began to levy a poll tax.[23]

Before the Civil War, some states used the poll tax to penalize free Negroes in various ways, although the payment of the poll tax carried with it no right to vote. A North Carolina law passed in 1749 required that all white males over the age of 16 were taxable while all Negroes, mulattoes, and persons of mixed blood to the fourth generation as well as all white persons who were married to any Negro, mulatto or person of mixed blood were taxable at the age of 12.[24] This discriminatory law does make it possible to identify free African American and Native American households in early North Carolina tax records when their female family members over the age of 12 were listed as taxable.[25]

In the 1830s and 1840s Georgia charged free persons of color a poll tax eight to 12 times the amount charged free white citizens. An 1824 Georgia tax list shows that a single white male was charged a poll tax of 31 cents while a free person of color was charged $4. In Tennessee, however, the state constitution exempted free men of color from the poll tax and militia duty as a sort of compensation for disenfranchising them.

In the 1890s and early 1900s legislatures in Southern states began to use the poll tax as a scheme to disenfranchise African-Americans as well as poor white citizens. States enacted laws to make payment of the poll tax voluntary but to use it as a requirement for voting. Florida imposed the poll tax as a suffrage qualification in 1889. Mississippi, Tennessee, Arkansas, South Carolina, Louisiana, North Carolina, Alabama, Virginia, Texas and

Georgia soon followed.[26] The poll tax payment was required up to a year in advance of any election, and voters were usually asked to produce the receipt for payment of the tax at the time of voting. Those who could not show the receipt were prohibited from voting. Georgia after 1877 and Alabama after 1901 required that all poll taxes for every year of voter eligibility be paid before voting was allowed.[27]

The poll tax was only one of several disfranchising measures including literacy tests and registration requirements that were adopted during this period.[28] After women won the right to vote by constitutional amendment in 1920, the requirement that they pay a poll tax kept many women from voting.[29]

Literacy tests were outlawed by the Civil Rights Act of 1964, which stipulated that anyone with a sixth-grade education was to be presumed literate. The 24th Amendment to the Constitution was ratified in 1964 and made it illegal for a state to use the payment of taxes as a voting requirement in federal elections. In 1966 the Supreme Court declared poll taxes as a qualification for voters in all elections unconstitutional.[30]

Poll tax records from the era of 1890-1964 continue to provide details on location of individuals for a series of consecutive years. The Alabama poll tax records, for example, include the registration date of the individual, his age at registration, and sometimes include the reason that payment stopped. W.C. Tierce of Tuscaloosa County, Alabama, registered and paid his first poll tax under the Alabama law of 1901 on 16 June 1902. The record notes his age as 38 years old. He paid $1.50 each year from 1901 through 1908. There is a final notation of his death under the remarks column indicating that he died presumably between 1908 and 1909.[31]

Research Example: Locate an Ancestor in a Specific County

Peter Rucker wrote his will on 18 January 1742/43 in Orange County, Virginia. A year later, on 29 February 1743/44, the will was submitted to the court for probate.[32] In his will Rucker left property to his sons Thomas Rucker; William Rucker; James Rucker; Ephraim Rucker; and daughters Elizabeth Pearce; Mary Offill; Margaret Tinsley and son-in-law Isaac Tinsley; and daughter Ann Cook and son-in-law Shem Cook. Reviewing the tax records may provide more information about these individuals and identify the spouses of the married daughters.

Table 7. Selected Tithables, Orange County, Virginia, 1739

Head of Household	No. of Tithables	Head of Household	No. of Tithables
Thomas Rucker	3	Ann Stogdill's Quarter	2
John Howard	1	Wm. Offill	1
Peter Rucker	6	Benj. Cave	5
Isaac Tinsley	1	Phillip Root's Quarter	15
Wm. Rucker	1	Wm. Carpenter	4
Wm. Pierce	1	Isaac Tinsley	1

Tithable lists for Orange County exist for the years 1736, 1739, 1756, 1772, and 1782. The 1739 list, a portion of which is shown in Table 7, is the closest in date to the will of Peter Rucker and is certainly worth checking. Remember that each male individual named in the tithable list would be responsible for his own head tax, plus any head tax due on sons between the ages of 16 and 21, plus any white servants over the age of 14 and any slaves over the age of 12.

In the 1739 list of tithables for Orange County, Peter Rucker was responsible for six tithables. Also listed in this tithable list are Thomas Rucker, William Rucker, William Pierce, Isaac Tinsley, and William Offill, indicating that they all lived within this district and were at least 21 years old. Shem Cook is not listed and may have been included in Peter Rucker's tithables. It is also possible that this young man did not yet live in this area in 1739 or was under the age of 21.

Head Taxes in Other Colonies

Pennsylvania used taxation to support its belief in the value of marriage and child rearing. The Quaker colony imposed a poll tax only on single men. Married men were charged a penny per pound (£) of valuation on both real and personal property but were not charged a poll tax. Those with a "great charge of children" and an estate worth less than £30 were given "due regard" by tax assessors who were free to negotiate the tax on an individual basis.[33]

In 1722 the North Carolina Assembly authorized its first tax, a poll tax, to finance the construction of a courthouse in each county.[34] Later legislation included head taxes for other specific projects:

- 1741: Empowered each court to impose for two years a tax of one shilling per poll for erection of a courthouse, prison and stocks, if not yet already built in county.
- 1741: Empowered the county court to levy a sufficient tax on each poll to provide for the purchase of standards for weights and measures.
- 1743: Authorized a one-time tax of eight pence for each poll for purchasing ammunition and renting suitable storehouses for it.
- 1748: Authorized an annual poll tax large enough to cover the cost of per diem allowances for men serving as jurors at the higher courts.[35]

In 1781 the Virginia Assembly passed a law that levied "a tax of ten shillings by every free male person above the age of twenty-one years . . . also upon all slaves, to be paid by the owners thereof . . . ."[36] The state of Virginia repealed the poll tax on white adult males in 1787, but the tax continued to be collected for county taxes, and tax collectors continued to record the number of white polls until 1850. Poll taxes continued to be levied on slaves by both the state and local tax authorities.[37]

Flat-rate taxes such as the poll tax were often criticized because they fell equally on the rich and poor. Maryland, in its Declaration of Rights in 1776, rejected the poll tax outright:

> *XIII. That the levying taxes by the poll is grievous and oppressive, and ought to be abolished; that paupers ought not to be assessed for the support of government; but every other person in the State ought to contribute his proportion of public taxes*

for the support of the government, according to is actual worth, in real or personal property, within the State[38].

Research Example: Separate Men with the Same Name in the Same County

Shem Cook was listed as a tax defaulter in Orange County, Virginia, in 1756. A search for a possible new location for Shem Cook after 1756 turned up a deed for land purchased in Amelia County, Virginia, by one Shem Cook. Fig. 6 summarizes the information extracted from *Amelia County, Virginia, Tax Lists, 1736-1764: an Every-Name Index*.

Cook	Cooke
Ben, 55f	Ben, 63k
Ben, 57b	Benja, 64w
Benja, 56f	Benjamin, 54f
Benjamin, 62f	John, 54f, 55d, 63k
Jno Jr.(dead, no effects), 63p	John Jr., 63k
John, 56f, 57b, 62f, 64a	Shem, 56f, 63k, 64w
John, Patroler, 55f	Shim Jr, 63k
John Jr., 55f, 56f, 62f	
Shem, 56f, 57b, 64a	*"56" indicates 1756*
Shem Jr. (no effects), 63p	*"f" designates the specific tax district*

Fig. 6. *Index for Cook/Cooke entries in Amelia County, Virginia, Tax Lists, 1736-1764: An Every Name Index, published by T.L.C. Genealogy, Miami Beach, Florida.*

The first listing in this index for any Shem or Shim Cook(e) is for the tax year 1756, indicating that he was in Amelia County no earlier than 1755. But in this tax index, there are two individuals named Shem Cook for the year 1756 (56f). They appear to be two separate individuals, both living in the same tax district. Which Shem Cook was the adult male who married Ann Rucker, the daughter of Peter Rucker, sometime before January 1742/43?

Since Shem Cook is listed in the index to the Amelia County tax lists, our next step is to look at the original records. In the tithable list for 1756 there is one household headed by John Cook, which included John Cook, Jr., and Shem Cook, who are assumed to be minors. The second Cook[e] household was headed by Shem Cooke and included two slaves named Dick and Jeney. This second individual appears to be the adult male who married Ann Rucker sometime before 1743.

In the original tithable list (Fig. 7), notice that the tax collector used curly brackets ({) to indicate household groups and added the number of individuals in the household. The brackets are invaluable in distinguishing family groups. Other tax collectors drew boxes around individual family groups.

The inclusion of Shem Cook in John Cook's household indicates that John Cook was responsible for paying for this tithable. Typically, a group listing included sons and perhaps other male relatives between the ages of 16 and 21, male indentured servants listed by full name, and slaves listed by first name only. Once a male reached the age of 21, he was moved to his own line and became responsible for paying his own tithable. The inclusion of Shem Cook in John Cook's household indicates that he was between 16 and 21 years old, and, therefore, must have been born between 1736 and 1740. The appearance of a second Shem Cooke on his own line implies that he was older than the Shem Cook listed in John Cook's household. There is also a reasonable chance that the elder Shem Cooke was related in some way to John Cook who named a son Shem. Further research confirmed that there

Fig. 7. Amelia County, Virginia, Tithable List, Thomas Tabb's District, 1756. Virginia Series 07780, Roll 1116. Courtesy of The Library of Virginia.

was a familial relationship between the adult Shem Cooke and John Cook.

Tracking Changes Through Tax Lists Over Time

One of the most important techniques in researching tax records is to track ancestors over a period of time. As you research all available records for a location over several years, you may be able to gather information about when your ancestor first arrived

Table 8. Study of John Cook Family Tithables,
Amelia County, Virginia, 1754-1763

	Households	No. of Tithables
1754	John Cook, Benjamin Cook, Jack, Hannah, Nann	5
1755	John Cook, Patroller, Benj. Cook, John Cook Junr., Jack, Hannah, Nann	6
1756	John Cook, John Cook Junr., Shem Cook, Jack, Hannah, Nann	6
	Benj. Cook	1
1757	John Cook, John Cook Junr., Shem Cook, Jack, Hannah, Nann	6
	Benj. Cook	1
1758	MISSING	
1759	MISSING	
1760	MISSING	
1761	ILLEGIBLE	
1762	John Cook, Jack, George, Dick, Tom, Lucy, Hannah	7
	Benj. Cook	1
	John Cook Junr.	1
	Shem Cook Junr	1
1763	John Cook, 1392 acres, James Cook, Jack, George, Lewis, Dick, Hannah, Lucy	8
	Benj. Cook	1
	John Cook Junr.	1
	Shem Cook Junr	1

in the county, when polls were added to his tax burden as his sons became taxable, and then when he lost polls as each son reached the age of 21 and became responsible for paying his own tax.

Research Example: Identify Men as They Become Adults

In colonial Virginia free white males became tithable when they reached their sixteenth birthday. At that time they were added to the tithable list of their father. When they reached the age of 21, they would be listed on their own individual line in the tax record. With the information in Table 8, you can calculate the approximate birth year for John Cook Junr. (1739), Shem Cook (1740), and James Cook (1747). You can also estimate that Benjamin Cook was born about 1735 because he is listed on a separate line in the 1756 tax records after being included in his father's household in 1754 and 1755.

Finding the Landless Ancestor

Poll taxes were continued in many states into the 1900s and were not limited to those in the South. Collecting poll taxes in Texas started during the days of the Texas Republic and continued after it became a state. The Arizona territory instituted a poll tax of $3 a year for every male inhabitant over the age of 21 in the 1870s.[39] California had a poll tax until 1913. These poll tax lists may enable you to locate and identify individuals who owned neither land nor personal property.

Research Example: Research A Landless Ancestor

Caesar H. Chapmond was born about 1858 to parents who were married in Sulphur Springs Township, Montgomery County, Arkansas, in 1854.[40] He was listed as a two-year-old child of Cezar

Chapman in the 1860 census of that township and county.[41] His father apparently died in Montgomery County in 1862 since letters of administration were issued for his estate in that year.[42] At that point, Caesar H. Chapmond disappeared from the records until his marriage to Emaline Jackson Burrows, a widow, on 19 October 1882 in Franklin County, Arkansas.[43] Caesar would have been 24 years old—fully of taxable age. You would expect to find a poll tax record for Caesar H. Chapmond in Franklin County, Arkansas, even if he did not own land.

The first step in the record search is to determine whether tax records for Franklin County, Arkansas, exist for 1879 and later. Franklin County tax records for 1879[44] as well as for 1882, 1884, 1886 and 1887[45] do exist. However, the records for 1879 do not indicate the presence of Caesar H. Chapmond. As a single young man who turned 21 in 1879, he was surely taxable but, because he had no apparent family ties in the county, he might have escaped the notice of tax collectors. Nor was he listed in the tax record for 1882, the year he married. The tax record for 1883, the year immediately following his marriage to Emaline Burrows, is missing. Finally in 1884 he was listed in the tax records with a single poll and no other taxable possessions. He was also listed in the tax records for 1886.[46] The record for 1887 for Franklin County, Arkansas, for his particular tax district is missing. Chapmond apparently moved back to Sulphur Springs Township, Montgomery County, Arkansas, between 1886 and 1888 because he was listed as a taxpayer in Montgomery County, Arkansas, for the year 1888.[47]

Poll Tax Records Can Replace the Census

Poll tax records generally list every adult male living in the tax district. These records are useful if the census is missing or if the individual reached taxable age before federal censuses began in 1790. They can also be used as a substitute for the 1890 census. Even if a census exists, tax records can confirm the location of an ancestor and may even add information not available in the census. Poll tax records are also useful in indicating the year when your ancestor arrived in the county or left the county between the decade years of the census. Tax records can also be used in this way to identify the year of arrival for immigrants to the U.S. as well. Remember that they would have been listed in the tax rolls in the year after their arrival.

---

[11] *National Genealogical Society Quarterly*, Volume 93, No. 1, March 2005, p. 64, cited by Elizabeth Shown Mills from "An Act, Supplementary to An Act to Regulate County Levies," Chapter XXI, *Laws of the Territory of the United States North-west of the River Ohio: Passed at the Second Session of the First General Assembly Begun and Holden at Chillicothe on Monday, the third day of November, one thousand eight hundred: with an appendix of resolutions*, Vol. 2 (Chillicothe: Winship & Willis, 1801), 69-70.

[12] Dora M. Whiteside, compiler, *Arizona Territorial Poll Tax Records, 1872-1876, Yavapai County, Prescott, Arizona* (Prescott, Arizona: Whiteside, 1984), Preface, iv.

[13] Nathaniel B. Shurtleff, editor, *Records of the Governor and Company of the Massachusetts Bay in New England*, 5 vols., Vol. 1:168 (Boston: 1853-54).

[14] Rabushka, "The Colonial Roots of American Taxation, 1607-1700," 68-69.

[15] Robin L. Einhorn, *American Taxation, American Slavery* (Chicago: The University of Chicago Press, 2006), 70.

[16] William Waller Hening, ed., *The Statutes at Large Being a Collection of All the Laws of Virginia from the First Session of the Legislature, in the Year 1619*, 13 vols. (Richmond, New York, and Philadelphia, 1819-1823; Charlottesville, Virginia: University Press of Virginia, 1969), 1:128.

[17] Hening, *Laws of Virginia*, 1:143.

[18] Hening, *Laws of Virginia*, 1:286.

[19] Hening, *Laws of Virginia*, 3:258.

[20] J. Christian Kolbe, "Colonial Tithables," Research Notes No. 17, Library of Virginia website, www.lva.lib.va.us/whatwehave/tax/rn17_tithables.htm : accessed 12 July 2004.

[21] Barbara Vines Little, abstractor, *Orange County, Virginia Tithables, 1734-1782, Vol. I* (Orange, Virginia: Dominion Marketing Research Corp., 1988), 41.

[22] "Poll Books," Research Notes No. 6, Library of Virginia website http://www.lva.lib.va.us/whatwehave/gov/va6_pollbooks.htm : accessed 15 May 2006.

[23] Richard Rose, *The International Encyclopedia of Elections* (Washington, D.C.: Congressional Quarterly, Inc., 2000), 208.

[24] Winslow, Jr., "Chapter 14: Tax and Fiscal Records," *North Carolina Research, Genealogy and Local History*, 232.

[25] Paul Heinegg, *Free African Americans of North Carolina and Virginia* (Baltimore, Maryland: Clearfield Co., Inc., 1997), Introduction.

[26] Frederic D. Ogden, *The Poll Tax in the South* (University, Alabama: University of Alabama Press, 1958), 4.

[27] Rose, *The International Encyclopedia of Elections*, 208.

[28] Ogden, *The Poll Tax in the South*, 31.

[29] Rose, *The International Encyclopedia of Elections*, 208.

[30] Harper v. Virginia Board of Elections, 383 U.S. 663 (1966).

[31] *Tuscaloosa County, Alabama, Poll Tax Records, 1901-1945*, microfilm no. 2,381,693, Item 2, Family History Library, Salt Lake City.

[32] Peter Rucker will, *Orange County, Virginia, Will Book 1, 1735-1743*; microfilm 0,033,000, Family History Library, Salt Lake City.

[33] Einhorn, *American Taxation, American Slavery*, 89-90.

[34] McCain, *The County Court in North Carolina Before 1750*, 110-111.

[35] Ibid.

[36] Hening, *Laws of Virginia*, 10:504.

[37] Einhorn, *American Taxation, American Slavery*, 49.

[38] Maryland Declaration of Rights and Constitution of 1776, online at http://www.lonang.com/exlibris/organic/1776-mdr.htm.

[39] Whiteside, *Arizona Territorial Poll Tax Records*, Preface, iv.

[40] Chapman-Brown marriage certificate, Oct. 1854, *Montgomery County, Arkansas, Marriage Records, 1851-1958*, microfilm no. 1,011,071; Family History Library (FHL), Salt Lake City.

[41] Cezar Chapman household, 1860 U.S. census, Montgomery County, Arkansas, population schedule, Sulphur Springs Township, page 925, dwelling 498, family 488; National Archives micropublication M653, roll 46.

[42] *Probate Records, 1845-1954, Arkansas Probate Court, Montgomery County, Arkansas, Vol. A-B, 1858-1903*, microfilm no. 1,011,078, FHL, Salt Lake City.

[43] Chapmond-Burrows marriage license, *Franklin County, Arkansas County Clerk, Marriage Records, Vol. BB-D, 1880-1891*, microfilm no. 1,034,244, FHL, Salt Lake City.

[44] *Franklin County, Arkansas, Persons and Personal Property Subject to Tax, 1879*, microfilm no. 1,027,884, Items 3-5, FHL, Salt Lake City.

[45] *Franklin County, Arkansas, Persons and Personal Property Subject to Tax, 1882, 1884, 1886, and 1887*, microfilm no. 1,027,885, FHL, Salt Lake City.

[46] Ibid.

[47] *Montgomery County, Arkansas, Persons and Personal Property Subject to Tax, 1881-1883, 1887-1888*, microfilm 1,011,092, FHL, Salt Lake City.

Chapter 4. Land Taxes

From Time Immemorial people have held land in return for some kind of fee – known at one time as feudal services, then as quitrents, and more familiar to us as real estate taxes. . .

Theresa M. Hicks, South Carolina Quitrents, 1772-1773-1774

The various methods used to tax land reflect differences in settlement patterns and social conditions in the American colonies. The type of settlement established, the distribution of land, and the taxation laws that followed were based on the political and economic needs of the developing area. Thus, the expansive and widely separated estates in Virginia did not lend themselves to direct oversight by assessors. In contrast, the villages of New England with their small fields and close proximity to neighbors were the perfect environment for strictly set rates and careful accounting.

Colonial Land Distribution

The Virginia Company made the initial permanent settlement in North America at Jamestown in 1607. The single men who first settled there were goldsmiths, glassmakers, silk dressers, perfumers, and those designated as gentlemen, none of whom was interested or experienced in cultivating crops. After the initial failure of early get-rich schemes that attracted these adventurers to Virginia, the survivors began to cultivate tobacco to make their fortunes. Land distribution became an important issue, and prominent men believed they were entitled to the large land holdings needed to grow the new "golden" crop.

In Plymouth Colony, on the other hand, the Pilgrims migrated to North America in family groups and staked a claim to the barren coastland that they held in common. Ten years later the Puritans arrived with a charter from King James and established the Massachusetts Bay Colony. They too held land in common for the first few years.

These colonies in New England were established by corporations chartered by the English king. The **chartered colonies** depended on financial support from the Crown and initially collected only quitrents, a land tax originally paid by freemen to the Crown or to the company that held a charter from the Crown. The quitrent, an annual payment of a fixed fee, secured a freeman's title to his land. It was paid in lieu of the services traditionally required by feudal custom.[48]

In the 1630s the Puritans in Massachusetts Bay Colony began to distribute land to individuals considered to be worthy members of the community. Initial land ownership was in small acreages in areas surrounding the central village. The towns started soon thereafter to tax this land, not according to its selling value but rather on the average income the land was thought to produce.[49] Both Massachusetts and Connecticut directed tax assessors to rate or value the land based on its use, quality, location, and position. These colonies also imposed different tax rates for different towns.[50] Taxation based on the quality of the land was subsequently adopted in several other states, notably Georgia, Tennessee, and Ohio.

Proprietary colonies, including Pennsylvania, Maryland, New Jersey, and Carolina, were initially granted by the King of England to proprietors who controlled vast land holdings stretching across whole colonies. In these colonies the proprietor owned title to all the real estate and needed to generate income by attracting settlers who would then pay taxes to the proprietor. Proprietors advertised for settlers and awarded generous headright grants. Lord Baltimore offered each free married man who paid £20 for his transportation to Maryland 100 acres of land with extra allotments for his wife, each adult indentured servant, and each child. Any individual who brought five more persons to Maryland received an additional 1,000 to 2,000 acres.[51] Other colonies, including Virginia and Georgia, offered similar headright enticements to settlers.

Land taxes in South Carolina were paid as quitrents throughout the colonial period, first to the Lords Proprietor until 1718 and then to the King of England after it had become a royal colony. The changeover in administration was an extended one; no quitrents were collected or recorded between 1718/19 and 1730. Therefore, the Act of 1731 required each landowner to file a memorial on his land describing when, how, and from whom he had acquired the land.

Dutch proprietors in New Netherlands (later New York) collected land taxes as a "tithe" amounting to one-tenth of the annual harvest following an initial 10-year tax exemption.[52] This followed a basic form of taxation in the ancient world, which was an assessment of a fixed proportion of agricultural produce.[53]

The Jamestown Colony in Virginia was originally established by the Virginia Company as a private enterprise chartered by King James I. To encourage immigration into the colony, the Virginia Company in 1618 authorized a provision that any person who settled in Virginia or paid for the transportation expenses of another person who settled in Virginia was entitled to receive 50 acres of land for each immigrant. King James I revoked the charter of the Virginia Company in 1624 making Virginia a **royal colony** but continued this headright allowance.[54]

The Crown required that owners of Virginia land pay a quitrent of two shillings for each hundred acres of land. If a landowner failed to pay the quitrent for a specified number of years, the Crown had the right to take back the land and grant it or sell it to another person. The money raised by this tax went into the royal treasury and was used to pay the expenses of the royal government in the colony.[55]

Using headright grants and large land patents to encourage settlement resulted in a comparatively small number of individuals owning most of the land. Not surprisingly, the Virginia General Assembly, composed almost entirely of large landholders, preferred to finance the administration of both the church and the colonial government through head taxes based on tithables rather than land taxes.

Land Taxes After the Revolution

It was not until 1782 that Virginia enacted its first true land tax by providing for a statewide enumeration of taxpayers on the county level for both land and personal property taxes. This law required each tax commissioner to prepare a list of the names of persons owning land or town lots, the quantity and value of land owned, and the amount of tax owed. By 1814 the assessment lists also had to include a brief geographic description including direction and distance to the courthouse.

Copies of annual tax lists of landowners for each county and independent city in Virginia from 1782 (or the date of formation of the county if after 1782) are available for research at the Library of Virginia. These records include those for "burned counties," providing important documentation for ancestors in areas commonly thought to have suffered major record destruction. The only exceptions are the years 1808 and 1864 when the Virginia legislature failed to authorize a real estate tax.

Ohio enacted land tax laws in late 1799 that taxed houses and lots in towns and rural mansions valued at $200. The land in rural areas was taxed separately based on the quality of soil. In 1800 first-quality land was taxed at 55 cents per 100 acres; second-quality land at 35 cents per 100 acres; and third-quality land at 17 cents per 100 acres.[56] Real estate taxes were eventually enacted in each territory as it was opened to settlement.

Tax Exemptions Used to Encourage Settlement

Governments in every period have used tax exemptions to reward certain actions or encourage specific behaviors. The original charter for the Massachusetts Bay Colony granted settlers an exemption from all royal taxes, subsidies, and customs for seven years and from all taxes for 21 years, except a five percent duty on imports into England.[57] Massachusetts and Connecticut granted exemptions to whole towns to enable the town to build a church or school. An exemption might also be granted if the town had suffered the ravages of an Indian attack or war.[58] At other times, exemptions were used to encourage necessary industry. In 1645 Massachusetts Bay Colony gave a company engaged in iron making a grant of land, a 10-year tax exemption, and a monopoly. In 1665 Connecticut granted a seven-year tax exemption to anyone setting up a forge.[59] During the Revolutionary War, Virginia exempted artisans employed at iron works from militia duty.[60] Virginia also used tax exemptions to encourage settlement of new counties. To speed settlement west of the Shenandoah River in newly created Orange County, the Virginia House of Burgesses enacted laws to exempt settlers from public, county, and parish taxes from 1734 to 1737.[61]

As American expansion proceeded after the Revolutionary War, cheap land and tax exemptions were often used to lure settlers to a specific territory. The federal government initially authorized the sale of land through cash entry sales in the Northwest Territory (later Ohio) in an attempt to raise revenue to reduce its Revolutionary War debt. Land sold for one to two dollars an acre while free military bounty land was granted to veterans of that war. The result of the federal government's land sales was an increase in settlement and a growing tax base for the individual territories. Prior to the 1850s those who purchased land from the federal government in Missouri, for example, were exempt from

Missouri land taxes for five years following their purchase. They were, however, taxed on personal property including livestock.

Tax Records Can Identify the Land and Location

In addition to the value of the land and the amount of tax due, real estate tax records routinely included a description of the land by section, township, and range numbers or watershed location, bordering neighbors, or former owners. In public land states, the tax districts themselves were identified by township and range, and the taxed land identified by section number and description (e.g., T1N R9E SE¼NW¼). Ohio land taxes were recorded either by rectangular land descriptions (township, range, section) or by entry numbers for land parcels in the various military bounty land districts. An 1851 California land tax list for the town of Sacramento is an alphabetical list of land owners with section fractions and lot numbers of town land owned. Land in Georgia was identified by district and lot number and was rated based on its quality (first, second, or third quality land), information that would not be available from the deed.

The 1850, 1860, and 1870 U.S. Census population schedules recorded the value of real estate owned by individuals. This is an easy way to identify individuals in specific counties who were landowners. But the value of the real estate was reported as a lump sum and does not indicate the number of acres, location, or quality of the land. Land tax records can provide information not found in other records. If the deed had not been recorded, the tax records may provide details about the property including its general location.

For example, according to the 1850 U.S. census for Georgia, Wiley Roundtree owned real estate valued at $3,500. The tax records indicate that he owned Lots 168, 169, 171, 181, 182, and 203 in Fayette County District 13, each 202-1/2 acres, totaling 1,215 acres. The tax records also indicate the quality of land for each property. Knowing the lot numbers also makes it easy to locate the property on a map.

Research Example: Separate Men with the Same Name in the Same County

We can use the combined land and personal property tax list of Westmoreland County, Pennsylvania, to try to separate several Applegate males living in the same county in 1787. To understand these tax records, we need to know that in Pennsylvania single men who owned no property paid a poll tax while married men were taxed on the value of their land and livestock. This poll tax was a penalty designed to encourage single men to marry and raise families. Except for the "single man" notation next to some names, the published index of the county tax records is of no help in separating men with the same surname.

> Applegate, Benj.
> Applegate, Benj. (single man)
> Applegate, Daniel
> Applegate, Garret
> Applegate, Jas.
> Applegate, Richard
> Applegate, Robt. (single man)
> Applegate, Samuel
> Applegate, Wm.
> Applegate, Wm. (single man)

The actual tax record for 1787 contains the notation that taxes collected in that year were due for 1785 and 1786. In other words, although all of these men were at least 21 in 1786, some of them might have been under 21 in 1785.

To sort out these several Applegate males into logical family groups, it is helpful to examine earlier tax records to see when each Applegate male was added to the tax list. The 1783 tax list included just four Applegate names—Benj. Applegate, Daniel Applegate, Wm. Applegate, and Samuel Applegate.

Table 9. Tax List, Westmoreland County, Pennsylvania, 1783

Name	No. of Acres	No. of Horses	No. of Cows	Value of Property (£.S)
Applegate, Benj.	300	2	4	184.15
Applegate, Daniel	275	4	6	197.00
Applegate, Samuel	0	1	2	16.15
Applegate, Wm.	300	3	5	198.00

This 1783 list indicates that three of these Applegates owned land while Samuel Applegate had none. From this information, you might hypothesize that Samuel was the youngest of this group, possibly a son of one of the older men.

According to the next available tax list, the one for 1787, the three Applegates who owned land in 1783 still owned it in 1787. The only change was that Samuel Applegate, who had previously owned no land, had acquired 85 acres by 1787. You could hypothesize that Samuel was the son of William Applegate based

Table 10. Tax List, Westmoreland County, Pennsylvania, 1787

Name	No. of Acres	No. of Horses	No. of Cows	Value of Property (£.S)
Applegate, Benj.	300	3	6	159.00
Applegate, Benj. Jr., single man	0	0	0	0
Applegate, Daniel	320	3	4	149.00
Applegate, Garret	0	2	2	13.00
Applegate, James	0	2	1	11.00
Applegate, Richard	0	1	2	6.10
Applegate, Robert, single man	0	1	2	8.00
Applegate, Samuel	85	1	3	54.10
Applegate, Wm. Sr.	200	3	4	147.00
Applegate, Wm., Jr., single man	0	0	0	0

on the report that in 1783 Samuel had no land and William had 300 acres while in 1787 Samuel had 85 acres and William had 200 acres. Neither Benjamin's nor Daniel's land holdings decreased. Deeds and probate records may provide additional information about the land these individuals had acquired.

Research Example: Use Tax Information to Lead to Other Valuable Records

A comparison of the tax lists for 1783 and 1787 also indicates a baby boom of Applegate males between 1762 and 1766 as several seem to have reached the taxable age of 21 by 1787. It will be necessary to do further research to separate these males into the appropriate family groups. A search of Revolutionary War pension applications for Applegates from Pennsylvania uncovered an application from Garrett Applegate, who gave his birth year as 1758. Garrett would have been taxable at age 21 in 1779 and liable for the poll tax levied on single men in Pennsylvania. His pension application, however, indicates that Garret enlisted four separate times to fight in the Revolutionary War and was in service through the end of 1783.[62] This explains why he does not appear on the 1783 tax list. Another Applegate, Robert, gave his birth date as 15 March 1759 in his pension application and also stated that he had enlisted five different times during the war.[63] Research in land records, wills, and probate records may provide more information about these families.

Delinquent Land Tax Sales

Even if you are unable to find a surviving record of tax collected, you may be able to locate records for delinquent tax sales. When the tax was not paid, the government would put a lien on the property and sell the lien to recover the amount it should have received in tax. The delinquent taxpayer had a period of time during which he could pay off the lien plus interest and clear the title to his property. If he did not pay this within the allotted period, the person who bought the lien would receive the title to the property. By 1843 there were laws in 19 of the 20 states that provided for summary tax sales when land taxes were delinquent.[64]

Notices announcing upcoming tax sales were published in local newspapers, often several times, to insure that all potential buyers were notified. The notices usually included the name of the delinquent taxpayer, the legal description of the property, and the tax due. The sale records themselves included a legal description of the land, name of the owner, amount of tax due, and the person who paid the back taxes to acquire the property. If you find an ancestor's name in a list of delinquent land sales, be sure to examine all the records to find out whether he actually lost the land or repaid the lien. In Iowa after 1860, farmers used these sales as a financing tool and often recovered clear title to their property. Iowa land owners had three years to redeem their property by paying the delinquent taxes plus a 30 percent penalty and ten percent interest per year from the day of the tax sale on both principal and penalty. The redemption period, the interest rate, and the penalty all varied by jurisdiction and time period.[65]

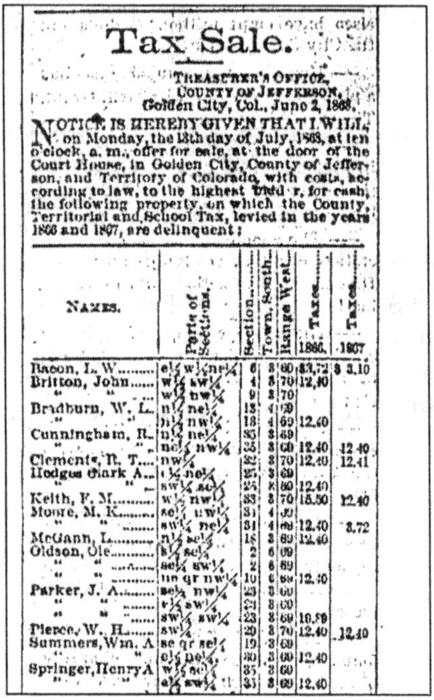

Tax Sale.

TREASURER'S OFFICE,
COUNTY OF JEFFERSON,
Golden City, Col., June 2, 1868.

NOTICE IS HEREBY GIVEN THAT I WILL, on Monday, the 13th day of July, 1868, at ten o'clock, a. m., offer for sale, at the door of the Court House, in Golden City, County of Jefferson, and Territory of Colorado, with costs, according to law, to the highest bidder, for cash, the following property, on which the County, Territorial and School Tax, levied in the years 1866 and 1867, are delinquent:

Names.	Parts of Sections.	Section	Town, South	Range West	Taxes 1866	Taxes 1867
Bacon, L. W.	e½ w½ ne¼	6	3	60	$3.72	$ 3.10
Britton, John	w½ sw¼	4	3	70	12.40	
" "	w½ nw¼	9	3	70		
Bradburn, W. L.	n½ ne¼	13	4	69		
" "	n½ nw¼	18	4	69	12.40	
Cunningham, R.	n½ ne¼	35	3	69		
" "	ne¼ nw¼	35	3	69	12.40	12.40
Clements, R. T.	nw¼	32	3	70	12.40	12.41
Hodges Clark A.	e½ ne¼	25	3	69		
" "	sw¼ se¼	25	3	69	12.40	
Keith, F. M.	w½ nw¼	33	3	70	15.50	12.40
Moore, M. K.	se¼ nw¼	31	4	69		
" "	sw¼ ne¼	31	4	69	12.40	3.72
McGann, L.	n½ se¼	18	3	69	12.40	
Oldson, Ole	s½ se¼	2	6	69		
" "	se¼ sw¼	2	6	69		
" "	ne qr nw¼	10	6	69	12.40	
Parker, J. A.	se¼ nw¼	23	3	69		
" "	e½ sw¼	23	3	69		
" "	sw¼ sw¼	23	3	69	10.89	
Pierce, W. H.	sw¼	20	3	70	12.40	12.40
Summers, Wm. A	se qr se¼	19	3	69		
" "	e½ ne¼	30	3	69	12.40	
Springer, Henry A	w½ se¼	35	3	69		
" "	e½ sw¼	35	3	69	12.40	

Fig. 8. Newspaper listing of properties to be sold for delinquent taxes. Golden City, Colorado Territory, 1868.

Tracking Delinquent Land Tax Sales Records

If you locate an ancestor's name in a newspaper notice of a pending delinquent tax sale, you can follow the trail in local government records. Be sure to note the legal description of the property to be sold: delinquent tax sales are usually indexed by legal description. Samuel Cobain, for example, was assessed $1.58 tax on lot 19, block 5, Buffalo Creek Park in Jefferson County, Colorado in 1892, which he did not pay. In the index to delinquent tax sales, first locate Buffalo Creek Park, then block 5 and then lot 19. You will find the number of the tax certificate for the sale, in this case No. 1228. In Colorado, tax sales are listed by certificate number in the Record of Delinquent Tax Sales. The entry for tax certificate 1228 shows that Robert Young purchased the lien at the tax sale and that Samuel Cobain paid $8.90 (delinquent tax plus interest) on 8 June 1893 to redeem the certificate and clear the title to his property. If, on the other hand, the lien holder gained clear title to the property, a notation to that effect was added to the record of delinquent tax sales.

Land Tax Records Can Point to a Migration Trail

Tax lists were prepared from the tax digests of the previous year. When the taxpayer failed to pay his taxes, he was marked as delinquent or added to the defaulters' list at the end of the current tax digest. Defaulters were not always miscreants trying to dodge the tax collector. Frequently, they were land or property owners who had simply left the area.

Faced with "missing" taxpayers who should, according to the tax lists, owe money to the county, tax collectors sometimes made notes indicating the reason taxes were not collected. In the 1894 tax list for Polk County, Tennessee, for example, the tax collector specified the destination of people who had left the county without paying the taxes due. As shown in Fig. 9, eight of the 14 taxpayers did not pay their taxes as indicated by the tic marks to the left of the numbers.

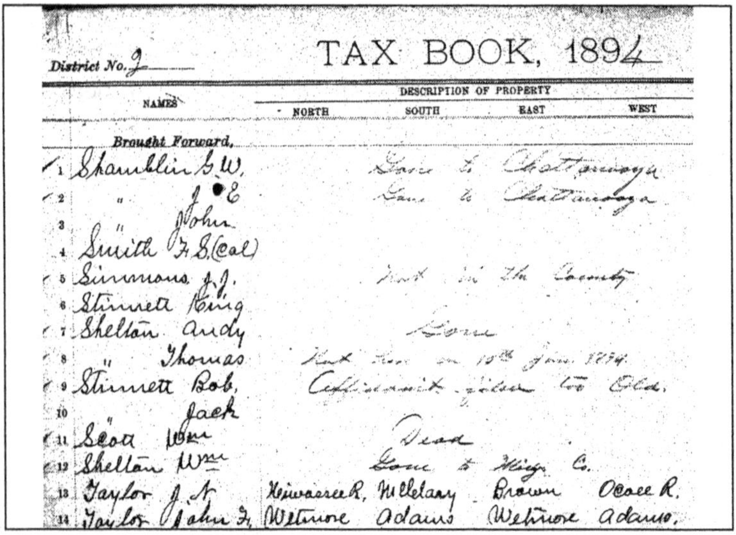
District No. 2 TAX BOOK, 1894

NAMES	NORTH	SOUTH	EAST	WEST
Brought Forward,				
1 Shamblin G. W.	Gone to Chattanooga			
2 " J. E.	Gone to Chattanooga			
3 " John				
4 Smith F. S. (Col)				
5 Simmons J. J.	Not in the County			
6 Stinnett King				
7 Shelton Andy	Gone			
8 " Thomas				
9 Stinnett Bob,				
10 " Jack				
11 Scott Wm	Dead			
12 Shelton Wm	Gone to			
13 Taylor J. N.	Hiwassee R.	McClary	Brown	Ocoee R.
14 Taylor John F.	Wetmore	Adams	Wetmore	Adams.

Fig. 9. Polk County, Tennessee, Dist. 2, Real Estate Tax List, 1894. Courtesy of the Tennessee State Library and Archives.

Land Holdings May Imply Arrival Date

Just as an individual's disappearance from the tax rolls may imply that he had left the county, so his appearance in the tax rolls may imply his arrival in a new location and provide additional information about his date of arrival. Tax records for the Republic of Texas report a number of individuals being taxed on 4,605 acres and 1,476 acres as well as the more common 1,280, 640, and 320 acres. Texas, originally colonized by Spain, initially used Spanish land measurements: league (4,428 acres) and labor (177 acres). After the Republic of Texas gained its independence from Mexico, it began making grants in 640-acre and 320-acre parcels similar to those in public land states. Table 11 shows the qualifying date of arrival and the amount of land received by families and single men for each category of headright granted.[66]

Table 11. Headright Categories in Texas

Category	Qualifying Date of Arrival	Amount of Land Grant to Families	Amount of Land Grant to Single Men
1	Before 2 Mar 1836	1 league + 1 labor (4,605 acres)	1/3 league (1,476 acres)
2	2 Mar 1836 – 1 Oct 1837	1,280 acres	640 acres
3	1 Oct 1837 – 1 Jan 1840	640 acres	320 acres
4	1 Jan 1840 – 1 Jan 1842	640 acres	320 acres

The 1840 Census of the Republic of Texas[67] is based on records of tax collection in 1840. By comparing the amount of land on which a man was taxed with the amounts available as a headright, you can form a hypothesis about his arrival date and even his marital status. Someone who was taxed on 4,605 acres, for example, probably arrived in Texas before 2 March 1836 and was married when he received his headright.

Tax Ledgers Arranged by Legal Land Description

Land tax research may prove difficult in states such as Alabama and Montana where land tax ledgers are arranged by the legal land description (Township, Range, Section) rather than by name of the landowner. Researchers will need to have the land description from the deed in order to research these records.

Additional Information Collected in Tax Records

Periodically tax collectors were instructed to collect additional information as part of their work. They might be asked to record the type of dwelling on the land being taxed, the materials used in the dwelling construction, or even the number of inhabitants. Pennsylvania tax records for the years 1821, 1828, and 1835 included the names and occupations of taxpayers as well as separate lists of free blacks, paupers, deaf and dumb persons, and tax assessors.

Beginning in the 1850s land tax forms grew more complex and required even more detailed information. The 1852 Georgia tax collectors were instructed to ask a one-time question concerning the number of persons subject to military duty in each household. Other states included lists of the names of militia members in the tax records.

With the growth of publicly financed schools in the 1840s and 1850s, tax collectors began to record the number of children in the household between the ages of 6 and 18 to ascertain the school-age population in the district. These lists are sometimes referred to as poor school lists because at that time schools supported with tax funds were called poor schools. Pennsylvania included the names of poor children in its tax lists as early as 1820, while Georgia tax lists began recording the number of school-aged children in each household in 1854.

Land tax records in Virginia can also help to date structures. Beginning in 1820 and continuing thereafter columns were added to the tax list to indicate the value added to the land due to improvements made to buildings on the property and the total values of the land and the buildings. An increase in the value of the buildings reported in this column from one year to the next may indicate the addition of a new building or improvements to an existing structure.[68]

Information Common to Land Tax Records

Information commonly found in land tax records includes:

- Name of owner and his residence;
- Type of ownership (whether held in fee simple, for life, homestead) as well as number of acres;
- Description of the land (on a water course, mountain, and contiguous tracts) or township, range, and section;
- Total value of the land;
- Amount of tax owed on the whole tract of land.

[48] Rabushka, "The Colonial Roots of American Taxation, 1607-1700," 67.
[49] Jones, *History of Taxation in Connecticut,* 16.
[50] *Connecticut Colonial Records*, Vol. VI, 338.
[51] Rabushka, "The Colonial Roots of American Taxation, 1607-1700," 71.
[52] Rabushka, "The Colonial Roots of American Taxation, 1607-1700," 72.
[53] Carolyn Webber and Aaron Wildavsky, *A History of Taxation and Expenditure in the Western World* (New York: Simon and Schuster, 1986), 71.
[54] Daphne Gentry, "Headrights," Research Notes No. 4, Library of Virginia online at www.lva.lib.va.us/whatwehave/local/va4_headrights.htm : accessed 6 June 2005.
[55] Daphne Gentry, "Taxes in Colonial Virginia," Research Notes No. 20, Library of Virginia online at www.lva.lib.va.us/whatwehave/local/va20_coltax.htm : accessed 6 June 2005.
[56] "Ohio Taxes Through Time," at www.ohio.gov/tax : accessed 5 February 2005.
[57] Rabushka, "The Colonial Roots of American Taxation, 1607-1700," 67.
[58] Jones, *History of Taxation in Connecticut,* 42.
[59] Rabushka, "The Colonial Roots of American Taxation, 1607-1700," 70.
[60] Hening, *Laws of Virginia*, 11:21.
[61] Scott, W.W. *A History of Orange County, Virginia: from its formation in 1734 (o.s.) to the end of Reconstruction in 1870*. Richmond, Virginia: E. Waddey Co., 1907, Chapter II.

[62] Garrett Applegate pension application file, *Revolutionary War Pension and Bounty Land Warranty Application Files*; micropublication M804 (Washington D.C.: National Archives).

[63] Robert Applegate pension application file, *Revolutionary War Pension and Bounty Land Warranty Application Files*; micropublication M804 (Washington D.C.: National Archives).

[64] Robert P. Swierenga, *Acres for Cents: Delinquent Tax Auctions in Frontier Iowa* (Westport, Connecticut: Greenwood Press, 1976), 10.

[65] Ibid., 22.

[66] Texas General Land Office, "Categories of Texas Land Grants," at http://www. glo.state.tx.us/archives/lgrants.html#headright : accessed 19 May 2006.

[67] Gifford White, compiler, *The 1840 Census of the Republic of Texas* (Nacogdoches, Texas: G. White, 1983).

[68] Conley L. Edwards, "Using [Virginia] Land Tax Records," Virginia Research Notes #1, Library of Virginia, http://www.lva.lib.va.us/whatwehave/tax/index.htm : accessed 5 June 2005.

Chapter 5. Personal Property Taxes

What is the difference between a taxidermist and a tax collector? The taxidermist takes only your skin.

Mark Twain, *Notebook*, 1902

Personal property tax records contain a wealth of information on the individual as well as on the community at large. Early personal property taxes were levied on livestock and vehicles. Gradually, luxuries such as stoves, clocks, some household furniture, gold and silver jewelry, and musical instruments were added to the list. Even items that we don't usually think of as personal property such as stocks and bonds, interest collected on debts, and cash on hand were taxed. Unlike real estate taxes, personal property taxes were levied on people at all levels of society.

Paying for Government

During the first 16 years of the Massachusetts Bay Colony, the General Court determined the total revenue needed to support the administration of the colony and apportioned that amount among the various towns, which collected it and remitted it.[69] Then in 1646 the court established a structured tax system it hoped would be "easy, equall, and certain." Cattle, houses, mills, ships and smaller vessels, merchantable goods, cranes, wharves, and all other visible estate at home or at sea were placed on the taxable

list. Livestock was rated individually based on the age and
condition of the animal.[70]

Virginia, on the other hand, began to tax personal property much
later. Beginning in 1782 the new state taxed white polls, black
polls (including slaves), horses, and cattle. There was no
assessment process since the taxes were a fixed amount per head.
There was also a carriage tax based on the number of wheels of
the vehicle. Table 12 is an example of a tax study of the Cooke
family of Gloucester County, Virginia.

**Table 12. Personal Property Tax List,
Gloucester County, Virginia, 1782**

Head of Household	White Males over 21	Slaves 16 and over	Horses	Cattle	Wheels
Giles Cooke Jr.	1	1	4	0	0
Thomas Cooke	1	5	2	0	0
Elizabeth Cooke	0	15	2	34	0
John Cooke	3	53	14	81	2
Mordecai Cooke Jr.	1	2	2	0	0
Giles Cooke of Fairfax Co.	0	3	0	0	0
Francis W. Cooke's Estate	0	16	4	19	0
Mordecai Cooke Sr.	1	22	13	41	2

It is obvious from this list that John Cooke, who was taxed on 53
slaves, 14 horses and 81 head of cattle, was by far the richest

Cooke in this district. Giles Cooke, Junr., and Mordecai Cooke, Junr., on the other hand, were apparently young men who owned just one or two slaves and a few horses. Giles Cooke of Fairfax County paid no poll tax in Gloucester County but was taxed on three slaves who were in this county. Elizabeth Cooke was apparently a widow, although not the widow of Francis W. Cooke. If she were the widow of Francis W. Cooke, her assets would have been included in the estate listing. She had no white males 21 years of age or over in her household but did owe taxes on the slaves, horses, and cattle that she owned.

Estates Are Taxable

This example also includes the estate of Francis W. Cooke. His estate appeared in the tax rolls of Gloucester County from 1782 through 1788. In the following year each heir was taxed on his separate portion of the estate, indicating that it had been settled. From this information you can hypothesize that Francis Cooke probably died shortly before 1782. The estate might have remained on the tax rolls for seven years because his widow remained in possession of the estate until her death or remarriage. Alternatively, legal disputes might have kept the estate open.

It is especially important to read the entire tax list for any year in which an individual disappears because there was no consistency in how estates were listed. You may find the estate listed simply as "Smith, John, dec'd." or as "Smith, estate of John." Sometimes an estate was listed under the personal name of the executor or administrator. The listing of an estate does not necessarily mean that an individual has died. In addition to probate estates, you may find estates for minors and for individuals who, for some reason or other, were not capable of administering their own affairs. Even if the estate were listed under another person's name, it would have its own line in the tax roll. Whenever you see multiple listings for the same name, you should consider the possibility that the individual is acting as an executor or administrator.

An unmarried woman was usually not listed in the tax records because of her limited legal standing. Unmarried women were included in the household of male relatives who would have been liable for the tax on her personal property. A widow's name may appear on the tax list after the death of her husband as the person liable for taxes on livestock, slaves, and poll taxes of adult sons.

Research Example: Establish a Year of Death As Estate Becomes Taxable

Based on the tax records of Maury County, Tennessee, Charnock Rust probably moved into the county around 1826 when he was

Table 13. Tax Study of Charnock Rust,
Maury County, Tennessee, 1837-1842

	District 6	No. of Acres	Value of Land	Land Tax	No. of White Polls	Poll Tax	Total Tax in cents
1837	Rust, Charnock	37	$300	0.330	1	0.375	0.705
1838	Rust, Avarilla	37	$300	0.450	0		0.450
1839	MISSING						
1840	Rust, Avarilla	37	$300	0.450	0		0.450
1841	Rust, Avarilla	37	$250	0.375	0		0.375
1842	Rust, Avarilla heirs	37	$300	0.810			0.810

first taxed. He continued to be listed in the Maury County tax records through 1830. The tax records for 1831 through 1836 are missing. Available tax records resume in 1837 when Rust was listed as the owner of 37 acres of land and charged for one white poll. The tax list for 1838 omits him but does include Avarilla Rust, who was taxed on 37 acres of land and no white polls. It is fairly safe to presume that Avarilla Rust is the widow of Charnock Rust, who probably died in 1837. Avarilla Rust continued to be listed in the tax records until 1842 when the inclusion of her heirs in the list suggests that she died about 1841.

Land and Personal Property Tax Lists Combined

The Cumberland County, Pennsylvania, assessment list for 1817 (Table 14) included the assessment on land, town lots and houses owned, horses, and cattle. The items on the assessment list shown

Table 14. Assessment List, Cumberland County, Pennsylvania, 1817

No. of Acres	Taxable Individual	Valuation ($)	Total Valuation ($)
	Christ, John Lumber Dealer	1,000	
26	Land, 2 houses ($80/acre)	2,080	
	2 Lots in Cumberland, unimproved	500	
	2 Horses ($60/each)	120	
	2 Cows ($20/each)	40	$3,740
	Cambel, John, Forgeman		
	2 Lots and 1 House	1,000	
	2 Cows ($15/each)	30	$1,030
	Cover, Jacob son of Gadson		
18	Land Timber ($65/acre)	1,070	$1,070

in Table 14 were obviously examined and evaluated individually. Cows and horses were rated differently as were the acres of land. The assessed value of each item was noted, and the list specified the number of houses on each property where tenants or relatives might live. Some records also provide additional information, such as individuals' occupations and some familial relationships.

Research Example: Estimate Wealth of An Ancestor

A 1795 tax list for Campbell County, Kentucky, provides information about the community and its individual taxpayers. By comparing the holdings of the individuals listed, we can determine the relative wealth of each. Mathias Corwin, who owned 450 acres of land, 12 slaves and 15 head of cattle, was apparently the wealthiest individual. We can assume that the same Mathias Corwin owned a town lot in Wilmington, Kentucky, because the tax collector made no notation to differentiate the two names. It is possible that Kezias and Joseph Corwin, who each

Table 15. Tax List, Campbell County, Kentucky, 1795

Names Chargeable with Tax	Total Blacks	Horses	Cattle	Acres	Water Course or Town	Town Lots
Corwin, Kezias		2	3	100	E. Fork Grassy Creek	
Corwin, Joseph		1	4	100	E. Fork Grassy Creek	
Corwin, Mathias	12	6	15	450	E. Fork Grassy Creek	
Corwin, Mathias					Wilmington	1
Cook, John	3	1	5	500	Licking	
Cox, John		2	1			
Crow, John					Wilmington	1

owned 100 acres of land in the same area, were his sons. You will want to do more research to identify the relationship among the Corwin individuals in Campbell County, Kentucky.

Property Tax Lists Expanded Over Time

Items taxed as personal property varied depending on time and place. Although slaves were considered personal property, they were not taxed as such but rather taxed "by the poll" or head. Initially, personal property taxed was limited mainly to livestock. Over time, county governments expanded the list of taxable personal property. Tennessee, for example, taxed carriages based on the number of wheels and taxed stoves as luxury items in the 1830s. In the 1840s Kentucky issued this list of tax rates to its tax assessors:[71]

- each gold watch, one dollar
- each silver lever watch, 50 cents
- each pleasure carriage or barouche, one dollar
- each buggy, 50 cents
- each piano, one dollar
- each pair of gold spectacles, 50 cents

In the 1850s in Georgia, a typical tax digest recorded a combination of land, slaves, white polls, and personal property as well as the number of school-age children. Information required included:

- number of white polls
- number of children, ages 8 to 18
- acres owned
- lot number
- value of real estate

- number of slaves
- value of slaves
- money on hand
- debts, mortgages held
- jewelry
- value of household goods
- value of livestock
- value of tools
- value of other taxable items
- total value
- poll tax due
- total taxes due

In 1867 Michigan expanded its definition of personal property to include "all goods, chattels, moneys, credits, and effects . . . all ships, boats, and vessels . . . all moneys at interest. . . all public stocks . . . all personal estate of moneyed corporations. . . and the income of any annuity."[72]

Arkansas tax ledgers for 1881 recorded property ownership in a number of categories including:

- number of horses; value of horses
- number of neat cattle; value of neat cattle
- number of mules and asses; value of mules and asses
- number of sheep; value of sheep
- number of hogs; value of hogs
- number of pleasure carriages; value of pleasure carriages
- number of gold and silver watches; value of gold and silver watches
- number of pianofortes; value of pianofortes

- value of goods and merchandise
- value of property required to be listed as banker, broker or stock on hand & jobber
- value of materials and manufactured articles
- value of moneys and credits and outstanding balances of book accounts
- value of moneys invested in bonds, stocks, joint stocks, joint stock companies
- total value of all other property required to be listed
- total valuation of personal property

In 1885 Arkansas began to include all types of wagons, not just pleasure carriages, and the gold and silver watch category was expanded to include diamonds and other valuable jewelry.

State Income Tax Replaces Some Personal Property Taxes

Personal property lists were based on self-reporting. Needless to say, underreporting was widespread. How would the tax assessor know about a diamond stickpin inherited from your uncle or the amount of money you kept under the mattress? As tax avoidance became tax evasion, tax collectors bemoaned low assessments and obvious omissions in the property lists. Personal property taxes also did not usually tax intangibles. In an effort to increase compliance, raise revenue, and tax intangibles, states began to experiment with the income tax, which soon became a more important source of revenue than the personal property tax. By the end of the 20th century personal property tax was being paid primarily on items that needed to be licensed, such as cars and boats, and on property used in a trade or business.

Homestead Exemptions Enacted

Homestead exemption laws were enacted in a few states as early as the 1840s to protect debtors from seizure of their homes and personal property to satisfy their creditors. The need for this sort of protection was reflected in the federal Homestead Act of 1862 that included the proviso that no lands acquired under the provisions of the Homestead Act were liable for any debts the settler contracted before being issued the patent on his homestead.[73] Fig. 10 is a property list prepared by C.I. Cooke to the court to obtain a homestead exemption.

To the Hon. The Court of Ordinary of Carroll County, Georgia

The petition of C.I. Cooke shoeth that he is a debtor and head of a family consisting of wife and eight minor children and claims the following property as exempt from seizure or sale under the laws of this state:

    One farm mill worth $100
    One cow and calf worth $20
    Ten head of hogs, fifty dollars worth
    Provisions and five dollars worth for each child
    Fifty bushels of corn, one thousand pounds of fodder, one horse
    wagon,
one table and set of chairs
Household & kitchen furniture worth $100
Beds and bedsprings sufficient for family
One loom, one spinning wheel, 2 pair cards, 100 pounds of lint cotton
Common tools of trade for self and wife
Ordinary cooking utensils and table, crockery
Wearing apparel for self and family
Family Bible, religious works and school books
Family portraits
One sewing machine.

                                        C.I. Cooke

Fig. 10. Homestead exemption petition prepared by C.I. Cooke, Carroll County, Georgia, circa 1883. Reproduced in Many Cookes and Their Broth by Charles G. Cooke, Arlington, Virginia, 1967.

In 1867 Michigan passed legislation giving each taxpayer an exemption for certain household goods including household furniture and stoves, spinning and weaving equipment, personal clothing, family pictures, books, and "to each householder, ten sheep with their fleeces, and the yarn and cloth manufactured from the same; two cows, five swine, and provisions and fuel for the comfortable subsistence of such householder and family for six months."[74] Court records often contain declarations of the property protected from seizure under the homestead exemption. These records provide a source of information about the valued possessions of individual families.

Personal Property Tax—"Everyman" Tax

Personal property taxes remain the best source for researchers to learn about the possessions owned by their ancestor as well as the wealth of the community he lived in. These records allow you to locate him in a specific area of a specific county, and to learn when he arrived in that location and when he moved away from that location even if he never owned any real estate.

---

[69] Douglas, *Financial History of Massachusetts*, Vol. 1, No. 4, 17-18.

[70] Shurtleff, *Records of the Governor and Company of the Massachusetts Bay in New England*, Vol. II:174-75.

[71] Milton Thompson, Sr., "Kentucky Tax Lists Have Useful Information," *Bluegrass Roots*, Fall 1985, 96.

[72] Russ Moore, "Personal Property Tax Law in Michigan," Informational Bulletin, State Archives of Michigan.

[73] A. R. Spofford, "Homestead and Exemption Laws," *Cyclopaedia of Political Science*. Ed. John Joseph Lalor. Library of Economics and Liberty. Maynard, Merrill, and Co. 1899. http://www.econlib.org/library/YPDBooks/Lalor/llCy544.html : accessed 29 May 2006.

[74] Moore, "Personal Property Tax Law in Michigan,"

Chapter 6. Federal Taxes

I am wholly unable to figure out the amount of the tax ... As this is a problem in higher mathematics, may I ask that the Bureau let me know the amount of the balance due?

Franklin D. Roosevelt, President of the United States
1938 letter to the IRS

Following the American Revolution, the individual states denied the power of taxation to the national government organized under the Articles of Confederation. The failure of the Confederation government, due in part to its resulting inability to raise money, led directly to the Constitutional Convention, which drafted specific guidelines for federal taxation.

> *Section VIII. The Congress shall have Power to lay and collect Taxes, Duties, Imposts and Excises, to pay the Debts and provide for the common Defense and general Welfare of the United States; but all Duties, Imposts and Excises shall be uniform throughout the United States.*

> *Section IX. No Capitation [head], or other Direct Tax shall be laid, unless in Proportion to the Census or Enumeration herein before directed to be taken. . . .*

These two sections provided the guidelines that Congress had to follow in drafting tax laws. Duties and excise taxes were limited only in that they had to be uniformly applied from state to state.

Section IX required that some taxes be collected from a state in proportion to its population. At the time the Constitution was written, poll taxes and real estate taxes were considered direct taxes. For these taxes Congress had to determine the total to be collected and then allocate part of the total to each state. In 1913 the ratification of the 16th Amendment changed the Constitution by eliminating the requirement that some federal taxes be proportional to population.

> *The Congress shall have power to lay and collect taxes on incomes, from whatever source derived, without apportionment among the several States, and without regard to any census or enumeration.*

There are three federal tax record groups that can provide genealogical researchers with specific tax information about their ancestors: the records of the Direct Tax of 1798; the Direct Tax of 1861 and its supplemental Act for the Collection of Direct Taxes in the Insurrectionary Districts within the United States; and the Income Tax of 1862-1872.

Direct Tax of 1798

The U.S. Congress passed the Direct Tax of 1798 to raise money to finance an anticipated war with France. The goal was to raise $2 million, apportioned among the states based on population as required by the Constitution. The act provided for the "valuation of lands and dwelling houses and the enumeration of slaves within the United States."[75]

For property valued at less than $100, no tax was due. For houses and outbuildings valued between $100 and $500 on less than two acres of land, the assessment was to be equal to two-tenths of one percent of the valuation. As houses increased in value, the tax rate increased up to one percent of the assessed value. There was also a provision in this act for a tax of 50 cents on each slave.[76]

The amount of tax money raised from taxing dwelling houses and slaves was then deducted from the total amount of tax due from each state. The remaining balance was to be raised by apportioning that amount among the owners of land that did not contain houses. The land tax list included the name of the owner or occupant; the quantity of each separate lot or tract of land; and description and dimensions of all wharves and outbuildings.

A variety of schedules were used to record the collection of the Direct Tax.[77]
- Form A—the "Particular List, or Description of each Dwelling House and associated outbuildings on a lot not exceeding two acres, but which property was valued at more than $100."
- Form B—the "Particular List, or Description of All Lands, Lots, Buildings and Wharves" except those already listed on Schedule A.
- Form C—the "Particular List of Slaves" including the names of the superintendents and owners of slaves, as well as the number of taxable slaves.
- Forms D, E, and F—"General Lists" that consolidate some of the same information found on Schedules A, B, and C.

- Forms G, H, I, and K—"Summary Abstracts" compiled from the General Lists.

Form A called for a variety of information about houses, outbuildings and land:
- name of occupant
- name of owner
- dwelling house or outhouse, appurtenances
- dimensions of structure
- materials of which constructed
- number of stories
- number of windows
- number of lights [glass window panes]
- number of houses claimed to be exempted from valuation
- number of houses admitted to be subject to valuation
- dwelling houses
- outhouses (actually outbuildings, such as a stable, kitchen, barn)
- quantity of land in the lots valued
- valuation of each dwelling house with the lot and outhouses by the assistant assessor.
- valuation of each dwelling house with the lot and outhouses by the principal assessor

Form A from Franklin County, Pennsylvania, (Fig. 11) lists George Brechem as the owner of a 22 ft. x 24 ft. one-and-a-half story log house. The house had four windows and 34 lights or panes of glass. This dwelling house, valued at £250, was situated on a lot that was 14,400 square feet or about one-third of an acre in Antrim Township. John Beashore had a two-story 28 ft. x 28 ft. log house

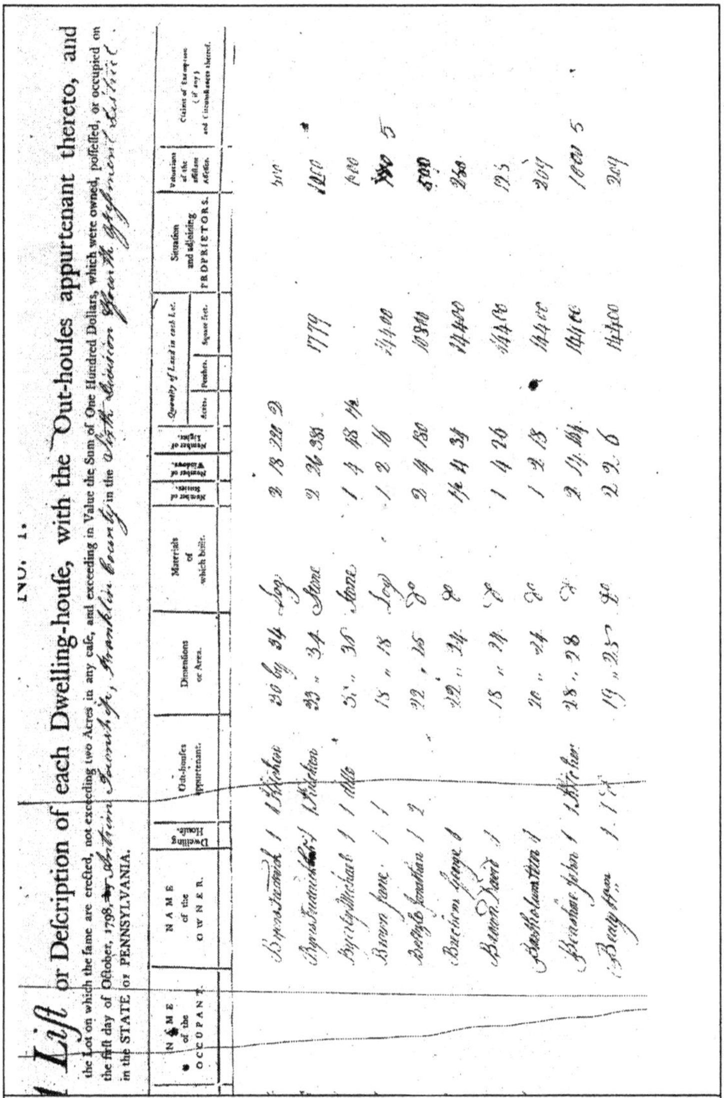

Fig. 11. A portion of Form A showing George Brecham on line 6 and John Beashore on line 9. Direct Tax of 1798, Franklin County, Pennsylvania. Washington, D.C.: National Archives, M372, roll 18.

with a separate kitchen outbuilding valued at £1000. The house had 14 windows and 164 lights.

Table 16. Some Records of the Direct Tax of 1798

State	Records Available and Location
Connecticut	Towns in the counties of Hartford, Litchfield, Middlesex, New Haven, New London, Tolland, and Windham at the Connecticut Historical Society
Georgia	Burke, Franklin, and Warren Counties at the Georgia Department of Archives and History
Maine	Hancock, Washington, Lincoln, Cumberland, York Counties at the New England Historic Genealogical Society
Maryland	Ann Arundel, Baltimore, Caroline, Harford, Montgomery, Prince George's, Queen Ann's, Somerset, St. Mary's, and Talbot Counties, and Baltimore City, at the Maryland State Archives
Massachusetts	Tax lists for most counties at the New England Historic Genealogical Society
New Hampshire	Transcript of District 13 consisting of towns of Alton, Brookfield, Effingham, Middleton, New Durham, Ossipee, Tuftonboro, Wakefield, and Wolfeboro
New Jersey	Transcripts of Hanover Township, Morris County; Lower Alloways Creek Township, Salem County, online at University of Delaware website
New York	Transcripts for Towns of Plattsburgh, Champlain, and Peru, in Clinton County, online; and Deer Park, published
North Carolina	Iredell County Land Valuation Book, 1800 at North Carolina Division of Archives and History
Pennsylvania	Entire state microfilmed at National Archives
Rhode Island	Towns of Providence, Richmond, Smithfield, and Warwick at Rhode Island Historical Society
Tennessee	Davidson County 13th Assessment District at Tennessee State Library
Washington, D.C.	Maryland Historical Society

Table 16 lists the states and counties for which microfilm of the original tax records or transcripts of the Direct Tax of 1798 are readily available. Direct Tax records for Pennsylvania have been microfilmed by the National Archives. Records for other states are in various local repositories. Microfilm of original records of Massachusetts, Maine, and southern New Hampshire are available at the New England Historic Genealogical Society. Some Direct Tax record transcripts for individual townships and towns have been published including *1798 Direct Tax New Hampshire District 13: consisting of the towns of towns of Alton, Brookfield, Effingham, Middleton, New Durham, Ossipee, Tuftonboro, Wakefield, and Wolfeboro*[78] and "Town of Deer Park [New York] 1798 Assessment Records."[79] Some transcripts are available online, including those for Hanover Township, Morris County, New Jersey[80]; Lower Alloways Creek Township, Salem County, New Jersey[81]; Towns of Plattsburgh, Champlain, and Peru, New York[82]; and portions of Berkeley Parish, Spotsylvania County, Virginia.[83] Many of these lists are incomplete or have been reconstructed from record fragments. It is possible that more original lists still exist, but so far they have not been located.

Tariffs and Import Duties

From 1790 to 1870 the federal government relied primarily on import duties for its revenue. During the first ten years of its history, the government collected $50.3 million (about 92 percent of its revenues) from duties on imports and from tonnage levies, while all other sources of revenue—including excises and other internal duties, postage, sale of public lands, and other miscellany—added up to just over $4 million.[84] Records of tariff and import duties, however, contain little personal tax information.

Direct Taxes of 1813, 1815, and 1816

The War of 1812 prompted Congress again to impose taxes to finance the war effort. There were excise duties on carriages, sugar refining, distilled liquor, and auction sales, license taxes on liquor dealers and retailers of imported goods, and stamp taxes. In 1813, 1815, and 1816 Congress also enacted several direct taxes on land, houses, and slaves designed to raise $3 million, $6 million, and $3 million respectively.[85] The amount was divided among the states in proportion to their population, but this time Congress authorized a 15 percent discount to states that collected the tax money themselves and paid it directly to the federal government. A majority of states took advantage of this arrangement, which spared the Madison administration the trouble of establishing an extensive bureaucratic infrastructure.[86] A few of these records still exist in local repositories, such as those in the possession of the Rhode Island Historical Society.

In 1815 the federal government also considered an income tax to raise an additional $3 million. The Secretary of the Treasury was of the opinion that this would be an indirect tax and, therefore, would not require apportionment. The war ended before such a tax could be enacted.[87]

Direct Tax of 1861

Fifty years later war again provided the impetus for enacting another federal direct tax. Congress passed legislation in 1861 to raise $20 million to fight the war against the secessionist Southern states. The legislation divided the amount to be raised by each state and territory including those of the newly formed Confederacy. Congress indicated that it had the right to tax all states including the insurrectionary states because they were technically a part of the United States in a condition of rebellion. The Direct Tax of 1861 "shall be assessed and laid on the value of all lands and lots of ground with their improvements and dwelling-houses. . . at the rate each of them is worth in money on the first day of April, 1862."[88] Under the provisions of the 1861 law, property valued under $500 was exempt from the tax. The law also provided that, if the tax were not paid, the tax assessor could sell the property. An allowance built into the law gave landowners two years to pay their debt plus a penalty of 50 percent of the tax per year of nonpayment.

The law required reporting of:
- name of the owner
- number of acres
- value of land
- amount of tax
- 50 per cent per annum penalty, if applicable

The federal government allowed the individual states to assume the direct tax and every jurisdiction with the exception of Delaware, Colorado Territory, and the Confederate states paid their quotas of the 1861 Direct Tax directly to the federal government.[89]

The following year Congress passed an Act for the Collection of Direct Taxes in the Insurrectionary Districts within the United States to create a mechanism for collecting taxes in Confederate states.[90] In the parts of states of the Confederacy that fell under federal control, the tax was levied and collected beginning in 1863.

Although the law exempted property valued under $500, tax lists included property well below that level. In the tax list for Anderson County, Tennessee, for example, Henry Taylor owned just 50 acres of land valued at $150. He was charged 53 cents in tax and a 27-cent late penalty.[91]

By the close of the Civil War almost all of the Union states and territories of the United States had met their specified apportionment of the Direct Tax, but it was only after the war ended that a real effort was made to collect the direct tax from most areas of the South. On 3 March 1865 Congress passed additional procedures for levying and collecting the direct tax in the insurrectionary states including the sale of land for unpaid taxes.[92] In 1866 the Committee on Reconstruction, in reporting the 14th Amendment of the Constitution to the Congress, recommended that any state government, upon ratification of this amendment, should be allowed to pay the state's share directly from the state treasury rather than collect the tax from individual taxpayers. The states would also be granted ten years in which to make the payment.[93]

Legislation in 1866, 1868, and 1869 limited further collection of the Direct Tax and after 1869 no further attempts were made to finish collecting this tax. Eventually the Supreme Court ruled that individual states could not assume responsibility for the debt and that individual citizens were responsible for paying the taxes. Congress then debated refunding the Direct Tax proceeds. Finally in March 1891 the Act to "credit and pay to the several states and territories and the District of Columbia all moneys collected under the direct tax"[94] was signed by President Benjamin Harrison. Delaware, one of only two states to collect the tax directly from its residents, required citizens to present original tax receipts to local authorities for a refund. Those lacking the appropriate 25-year-old paperwork were not paid. The Delaware Public Archives has a collection of manuscript records of individual claims for refunds of the 1861 Direct Tax.

The National Archives has microfilmed copies of the Civil War Direct Tax Assessment Lists for Tennessee (RG 217, T227, 6 rolls). NARA also maintains textual records dealing with the collection of the Direct Tax of 1861 and its aftermath, including:

- Applications to redeem land sold for taxes
- Tax sales certificates
- Correspondence dealing with the collection of the Direct Tax of 1861

Appendix A contains a complete list of textual records available at the National Archives regarding the Direct Tax of 1861.

One result of the 1862 law regarding collection of direct taxes in the insurrectionary districts was the acquisition of Arlington House, the centerpiece of Arlington National Cemetery. The house had been willed to Mary Anna Randolph Custis by her father, George Washington Parke Custis, the adopted grandson of George Washington. When Mary Ann married Robert E. Lee, he became the custodian of the property although the house belonged to Mary Ann. She sent an agent to pay the tax, which was refused by the collection agent because she did not appear in person. The 1,100-acre property was seized by the federal government, offered for public sale on 11 January 1864, and purchased by a tax commissioner for government use.

Brig. Gen. Montgomery C. Meigs established the property as a military cemetery in 1864; his intention was to render the house uninhabitable. The Lees never returned, but after the death of Robert E. Lee in 1870, his eldest son, George Washington Custis Lee, brought suit in the Circuit Court of Alexandria (today Arlington) County, Virginia. He claimed that the land had been illegally confiscated and that he was the legal owner. In December 1882, the U.S. Supreme Court, in a 5-4 decision, returned the property to Lee, stating that it had been confiscated without due process. On 3 March 1883, Congress purchased the property from Lee for $150,000.[95]

Federal Income Taxes (1862-1872)

The Internal Revenue Act of 1 July 1862 was intended "to provide Internal Revenue to support the Government and to pay Interest on the Public Debt."[96] This annual tax was imposed on all income in excess of $600. Legacies and distributive shares of personal property were also taxed. Taxes were levied on manufacturers producing a wide variety of products ranging from ale to zinc. Monthly taxes were levied on the gross receipts of transportation companies; on interest paid on bonds; on surplus funds accumulated by financial institutions and insurance companies; on gross receipts from auction sales; and on sales of slaughtered cattle, hogs, and sheep. Annual license fees were required for all trades and occupations, and annual duties were placed on carriages, musical instruments, gold and silver jewelry. Most surprising of all, stamp taxes were levied on legal and business documents, medical preparations, playing cards, perfumes and cosmetics.[97] The tax credited with moving the colonies toward revolution was now imposed to finance the Civil War.

In Table 17, a list of selected Internal Revenue Tax Assessments for the Colorado Territory, notice that George David reported $267 in income from his furniture manufacturing business, and Howard Colony reported income of $443 from his jewelry manufacturing business. The tax rate was set at three percent on manufacturers. In addition, people who had licenses, including peddlers and hotelkeepers, were charged a tax on the license in addition to any local fee required to secure the license.

**Table 17. Selected Internal Revenue Tax Assessments,
Colorado Territory, 1863**

Name	Town	Occupation/ Business	Income	Tax
Stolz, Schmaker	Black Hawk	Saddlery	$793	$23.79
Colony, Howard	Central City	Jewelry Mfg.	$443	$13.35
Harley, Benj.	Mt. Gulch	Peddler	License	$13.75
David, George	Denver	Furniture Mfg.	$267	$8.01
Hamilton, T.R.	Central City	Furniture Mfg.	$552	$16.56

At the end of the Civil War, internal revenue taxes were instituted for southern states. Individuals subject to income tax included physicians, lawyers, blacksmiths, hotelkeepers, manufacturers of furniture, jewelry, saddles, and other tangible goods. Annual licenses were required for all trades and occupations, and an annual tax duty was levied on carriages, yachts, billiard tables, and gold and silver plate. The 1864 change to the internal revenue assessment law set the tax rate at five percent on all incomes, even those under $600. Amendments passed in 1866 set the rate at five

Table 18. Selected Internal Revenue Tax Assessments, Georgia Division 4, Collection District 4 including Atlanta, 1866

Name	Location	Article or Occupation	Quantity or Valuation	Rate of Tax	Amount of Tax	Total Tax ($)
Pegg, Samuel	Atlanta	carriage	1	1.00	1.00	
		watch	2	1.00	2.00	3.00
Roberts, M.L.	Alabama	retail liquor dealer	Sec. 12	25.00	25.00	
		income	$664.53	5%	33.22	
		watch	2	1.00	2.00	60.22
Rogers & Castleberry		retail liquor dealer	Sec. 12	25.00	25.00	25.00
Richards, A.M.		hotel	Sec. 12	30.00	30.00	30.00
Robinson, G.M.	Whitehall Ga.	lawyer	Sec. 12	10.00	10.00	10.00

Source: Internal Revenue Assessment Lists for Georgia, 1865-66. Record Group 58, M762, roll 7 (Washington, D.C.: National Archives).

percent on incomes over $600 and ten percent on incomes over $5,000. The first federal income tax was extended through 1872.

Appendix B contains a complete list of microfilmed records of the Internal Revenue Assessment Records for the period 1862-1872.

Confederate Taxes

At the start of the Civil War the Confederacy also found itself in need of money. It was unable to borrow enough to support its war efforts because the region's wealth was in land and slaves rather than liquid assets or manufactured goods. Early efforts to raise revenue through taxes were ineffective, in part because the Confederacy had to make requests of the individual states for funds. The states in turn had to voluntarily collect and remit those taxes. Many states simply did not collect taxes, preferring to raise revenue by borrowing, issuing bonds, printing their own currency, or a combination of these methods.

Eventually, the Confederacy was forced to enact tax legislation and on 24 April 1863 passed a tax package that included a progressive income tax, excise taxes, license fees, a ten percent tax on wholesalers, and a ten percent tax-in-kind on agricultural products.[98] Most of these taxes were collected at the local level and remitted to the Confederate government. Records of these collections may be located with other county tax records or may be in a state repository.

The tax-in-kind allowed the Confederacy to collect commodities that were needed to support its troops. Farmers were allowed to keep specified quantities of produce for their own use. After setting aside these reserves, they were required to deliver ten percent of the remaining crops, including wheat, sweet and Irish potatoes, cotton, tobacco, and wool to Confederate quartermasters.[99] Fig. 12 is an example of a Confederate tax notice listing the items to be taxed.

Tax assessors were instructed to estimate the quantity, quality, and value of each farmer's crops. In cases of disagreement between the tax assessor and the farmer, each was to select a freeholder of the neighborhood to resolve the disagreement. Assessors then provided information about collected commodities to the army quartermasters. Most of the produce went to army supply points to be distributed to the troops. Cotton and tobacco,

The taxpayers of Orange county are hereby notified to attend at the times and places above stated nearest their respective residences, and furnish to the Assessors a correct list of the following subjects of taxation on hand, held or owned on the 17th of February, 1864: Number of acres of Land, and value in 1860; slaves, number, sex and value; number of Horses, Mules, Asses, Jennets, Cattle, Sheep, Goats and Hogs, value in 1860; Cotton, Wool, Tobacco[,] Corn, Wheat, Oats, Rye, Potatoes, Peas, Beans, &c., Flour, Meal, Sugar, Molasses, Bacon, Lard, Spirituous Liquors &c., on hand 17th February, 1864, and not necessary for family consumption in 1864; Household and Kitchen Furniture, Agricultural Implements, Mechanical Tools, Musical Instruments, Carriages, Carts, Drays, Wagons, Books, Maps, and value in 1860; Property of Corporations, joint Stock Companies and Associations, Gold and Silver Coin, Gold Dust, and Gold and Silver Bullion; amount of all solvent Credits, Bank Bills, and all other paper issued as currency; value of money held abroad, and bills of exchange in foreign countries, and the value of all articles of primal or mixed property not enumerated above, and not exempt from taxation.

Land, Slaves, Cotton and Tobacco purchased since the 1st day of January 1864, must be listed at the amount paid for them.

Notice Issued at Orange County, North Carolina

Fig. 12. Confederate tax notice, Orange County, North Carolina, 1864. Used with permission of the Documenting the American South Project, The University of North Carolina at Chapel Hill Libraries. http://docsouth.unc.edu/imls/orcotax/tax.html

however, went to agents of the Confederate Treasury for sale. Quartermasters also had the option of selling crops that might spoil and, if it were not practical to collect the produce, could collect the tax in currency.[100]

Records generated by this tax include receipts to the assessors, notices concerning the location and time for crops to be turned over, lists of taxpayers and the crops turned in, and estimates of the quantity and quality of the crops. Unfortunately, these records are scattered and incomplete. Some quartermasters took their records with them at the end of the war so you may find them in manuscript collections of personal papers. Some are in county historical society collections or in state archives. Some, of course, were destroyed.

Tariffs Decline in Significance

The tariff on manufactured goods imported into the U.S. after the Civil War helped to protect and subsidize domestic manufacturing and paid off a substantial portion of the Union Civil War debt. But as the Industrial Age gathered steam, America became an exporter rather than an importer of manufactured goods, and the collection of tariffs declined. Although opposed by wealthy northern industrialists, the movement for an income tax became stronger in the years after 1880 as the federal government sought new sources of revenue.

Income Tax Reconsidered

In the 1880s a movement began urging Congress to replace high customs duties with an income tax, but Congress initially rejected the plan. In 1894 Congress finally passed an income tax on all incomes in excess of $4,000 at a rate of two percent. Because of what was considered a high threshold of $4,000, 98 percent of the people were exempt. Within a year, the Supreme Court struck down the law as unconstitutional because it was deemed a direct tax that was not being apportioned among the states based on population as required by the Constitution. This decision eventually led to the writing of the 16th Amendment to the U.S. Constitution.

The most familiar federal tax records created in the 20th century are income tax records. Although these were considered public records until 1977, they were open to inspection only under

Treasury Department regulations approved by the President or by presidential order. The government also considers income tax returns to be temporary so most have been destroyed.

Tax Protests

Tax protests in America were not limited to riots against the Stamp Act of 1765 or the Boston Tea Party in 1773 and did not end with the American Revolution. In 1786 Massachusetts' enactment of a tax to pay debts accumulated during the Revolutionary War triggered a rebellion. Many in the western part of the state were unable to pay their taxes and were prosecuted and jailed for their failure. Daniel Shays led an army of 1,000 men that closed down the Massachusetts Supreme Court and liberated imprisoned debtors. Wealthy Bostonians contributed money to pay soldiers to put down the rebellion in the west, which they did in a brief skirmish in January 1787. Shays escaped to Vermont but 150 of his men were captured and sentenced to death.[101] Pardons were eventually granted, but the episode convinced many of the need for strengthening the central government and improving mechanisms for collecting taxes.[102]

The Whiskey Rebellion in 1794 was a reaction to a government-imposed excise tax on the manufacture of whiskey. Farmers in western Pennsylvania distilled their corn into liquor, which was used as a form of barter. Secretary of the Treasury Alexander Hamilton declared that liquor was a luxury item and therefore should be taxed as such. Frontiersmen refused to pay the tax and attacked collectors who tried to collect it. The federal government under George Washington was alarmed by the widespread tax revolt and ordered the militia of Pennsylvania to put it down.

About 50 individuals were arrested for resisting the tax; only two were found guilty and both were eventually pardoned. The results were positive for the infant federal government. The insurrection was put down, overt resistance ended, and taxes were collected.[103]

Perhaps the most familiar tax protest was over the counting of window panes required by the Direct Tax of 1798. The counting of windows was a small part of the enumeration of property by type of building material, types of outbuildings, and amount of land. But the counting of glass panes in each window caused a noisy protest among German farmers in western Pennsylvania. The modest 648-square-foot log home of William McClelland of Antrim Township, Franklin County, Pennsylvania, had just two windows that included eight panes of glass. But John McLenahan's 720-square-foot, two-story brick building in the same township included 15 windows with 234 lights.

Tempers rose among these Pennsylvania farmers as assessors stood and counted the number of panes of glass in each window. There were reports of housewives pouring buckets of boiling water down onto assessors, and some assessors reported death threats. Rumors spread that the number of lights were being counted as the basis for future taxes.

In the Pennsylvania counties of Northampton, Bucks, and Montgomery, German farmers, incited by an auctioneer named John Fries, forcefully resisted the efforts of the assessors to evaluate their property. On 20 March 1799, the U.S. Secretary of War directed the governor of Pennsylvania to call out troops to quell the insurrection. The state militiamen marched into the rebellious counties on April 4, and a stern directive to cease and desist was issued.

The cease and desist order issued by Brig. General William MacPherson to the German residents reminded them that the tax rate was modest and pointed out that higher rates were being charged only on those most able to pay. His proclamation continued:

> *As a further proof of the attention of Congress to the wishes and accommodations of the people, they have, during the last session, repealed that part which required a statement of the windows of each dwelling house, and which, as it afterward appeared, was more disagreeable than necessary or useful. Therefore no further account of the windows has been demanded.*[104]

MacPherson went on to point out, "This act is not perpetual, being only for one year, and will not be continued unless the public good demands it."[105]

Shortly thereafter Fries and 30 other men were captured in Bucks County. Fries was tried and convicted of treason and sentenced to death; President John Adams eventually pardoned Fries and two others convicted in the uprising.

Henry David Thoreau is perhaps the most famous individual tax protester in America for refusing to pay the Massachusetts poll tax of $1.50 in 1845. He had apparently been delinquent since 1842, but was jailed on 23 July 1846 for nonpayment. Thoreau wrote that he wished never to "rely on the protection of the State," and therefore did not wish to pay for its support. He was released after a relative paid the tax for him over his objection.[106]

Tax Assessors and Collectors

Many governments throughout the ages have recognized the difficulty of extracting money from the population. Collections were frequently assigned to independent contractors or "tax farmers" who collected taxes in return for a percentage of the take. Governments therefore did not have to employ tax collectors while benefiting as the funds collected were added to their treasuries. Tax collectors employed a variety of methods to extract the maximum amount of tax ranging from threats of prosecution to physical violence.

From the beginning in Massachusetts, the constable collected taxes because he was armed and already had the power to arrest people if duress was necessary. In Virginia it was the sheriff, someone entrusted to keep the peace and exert authority over the community, who collected taxes. As expenses exceeded collections in Massachusetts, the General Court expressed its conviction as early as 1646 that the constables, marshals, auditor or treasurer were to blame for low collections, and a committee was selected to investigate and prosecute the delinquents.[107] Eventually, the poor performance of the tax assessors in Massachusetts in the period after 1692 led to the adoption of laws governing their appointment and performance. Several laws were passed requiring oaths for assessors, property qualifications, penalties on towns for not electing assessors, and penalties on assessors for not serving when elected. The Assembly authorized assessors to require lists of property from inhabitants, and stipulated penalties on inhabitants for not furnishing taxable property lists to assessors.[108]

Likewise, when Virginia collections fell far short of expenses, the House of Burgesses passed a series of laws beginning in 1691 that attempted to force sheriffs to present their tax records for audit; these laws were ignored.[109] Other colonies enacted similar laws in order to ensure the flow of tax money into government coffers.

Collecting taxes was frequently a face-to-face process before the 20th century. Tax collectors sat at the church door in colonial Virginia to collect the tithable lists. Excise tax collectors were assigned to observe merchants and tradesmen to determine the amount of their production. Tax assessors stood in the yard of each house and counted the windows as part of the assessment for the Direct Tax of 1798. Toll roads were often used to inspect and tax commodities going to market. Revenuers searched along back roads for moonshiners who were trying to dodge the federal excise tax on liquor manufacture.

For engaging in one of the most dangerous of occupations, tax assessors and collectors often received a percentage of their collections. This system encouraged diligent and sometimes abusive collection methods as well as hostility and violence on the part of some of the population. In the 20th century, the urbanization of the workforce, the rapid growth of population, and the computerization of records have made a more impersonal collection system possible.

[75] *Statutes at Large of the United States of America, 1789-1873, 17 vols.,* 1:597.

[76] *U.S. Stats at Large,* 1:598.

[77] Description of forms provided by the Pennsylvania State Archives website, http://www.phmc.state.pa.us/BAH/DAM/census.htm : accessed 12 August 2006.

[78] John S. Fipphen, *1798 Direct Tax New Hampshire District 13 consisting of the towns of Alton, Brookfield, Effingham, Middleton, New Durham, Ossipee, Tuftonboro, Wakefield, and Wolfeboro* (Bowie, Maryland: Heritage Books, 1989).

[79] "Town of Deer Park [Suffolk County, New York] 1798 Assessment Records," *Orange County [NY] Historical Society Publication No. 8* (Goshen, New York, 1978-79), 13-25.

[80] Transcript of Direct Tax of 1798 for Hanover Township, Morris County, New Jersey, Center for Historic Architecture & Design, University of Delaware School of Architecture, http://dspace.udel.edu:8080/dspace/handle/19716/1337 : accessed 15 December 2006.

[81] Transcript of Direct Tax of 1798 for Lower Alloways Creek Township, New Jersey, University of Delaware, http://dspace.udel.edu:8080/dspace/handle/19716/1341 : accessed 15 December 2006.

[82] Transcript of Direct Tax of 1798 for Plattsburgh, Champlain, and Peru, New York at US Genweb Project, Clinton County, New York, Rootsweb.com, http://www.rootsweb.com/~nyclinto/1798tax.html : accessed 15 December 2006.

[83] Transcript of Direct Tax of 1798 for Berkeley Parish, Spotsylvania County, Virginia, University of Mary Washington, Department of Historic Preservation, http://departments.umw.edu/hipr/www/1798l2b.htm : accessed 15 December 2006.

[84] *American State Papers: Finance,* Washington: Gales and Seaton, 1832-1861, 1:665.

[85] *U.S. Stats at Large,* 3:53, 164, 255

[86] Tax History Museum at http://www.tax.org/Museum/1777-18.15.htm : accessed 12 December 2005.

[87] Ibid.

[88] *U.S. Stats at Large,* Vol. 12, Chap. 45, Sec. 13, 297.

[89] Einhorn, *American Taxation, American Slavery,* 158.

[90] *U.S. Stats at Large,* Vol. 12, Chap. 98, 422.

[91] "Assessment Lists of the United States Direct Tax Commission, Tennessee," Records of the Accounting Officers of the Department of the Treasury, RG 217, T227, Roll 1, Anderson County, Tennessee. Washington, D.C.: National Archives.

[92] Smith, *A Genealogy Miscellany, Henderson County[Tennessee] III,* 68-70.

[93] Ibid.

[94] 26 *U.S. Stats at Large,* 822-823.

---

[95] "Arlington House," Arlington National Cemetery: Historical Information http://www.arlingtoncemetery.org/text/arlington_house_text.html : accessed 25 May 2005.

[96] *U.S. Stats at Large*, 12:432.

[97] Claudine J. Weiher, "Introduction," Internal Revenue Assessment Lists for Georgia, 1865-66. National Archives Record Group 58, M762, roll 7.

[98] 1st Congress C.S.A., Stat. 122-125

[99] Henry Putney Beers, *The Confederacy: a Guide to the Archives of the Government of the Confederate States of America* (Washington, D.C.: NARA, 1986), 166-170.

[100] Ibid.

[101] Shays's Rebellion, U.S. History.com, http://www.u-shistory.com/pages/h363.html : accessed 7 March 2005.

[102] Einhorn, *American Taxation, American Slavery*, 53.

[103] Forsythe, *Taxation and Political Change in the Young Nation, 1781-1833*, 50.

[104] MacPherson's letter quoted by Judith Ann Meier, "The Federal Direct Tax of 1798: The Window Pane Tax," *The Bulletin of HSMC*, published by the Historical Society of Montgomery County, Pennsylvania, Vol. 22, 358.

[105] Ibid.

[106] Henry David Thoreau, "On the Duty of Civil Disobedience," *The Essays of Henry D. Thoreau* (New York: North Point Press, 2002).

[107] Douglas, *Financial History of Massachusetts*, Vol. 1, No. 4, 24.

[108] Ibid., 61.

[109] Hening, *Laws of Virginia*, 3:48.

Chapter 7. Inheritance and Estate Taxes

The difference between death and taxes is death doesn't get worse every time Congress meets.

Will Rogers, American humorist

The colonial, state, and federal governments have all used probate fees, inheritance taxes, and estate taxes to raise revenue. A variety of wealth transfer taxes were established, and some definitions are in order.

- A probate fee is imposed when an estate is settled by the court. It may be either a flat rate or a graduated rate so that larger estates pay higher fees.
- An estate tax is levied against the estate left by a deceased person based on the value of the estate after allowable deductions.
- An inheritance tax is a tax on the right to inherit any type of property.
- A legacy tax is a tax on the right to inherit personal property.
- A succession tax is a tax on the right to inherit real property.

Federal Estate and Inheritance Taxes

In 1794 a special revenue committee of the House of Representatives recommended a system of stamp duties that included a probate fee on the estate of a deceased individual. The Stamp Act of 6 July 1797 imposed a fee on receipts of legacies and shares of personal property valued at more than $50. The fee ranged from 25 cents for a legacy valued between $50 and $100 and 50 cents for a legacy between $100 and $500. An additional one dollar was charged for each additional $500 of value of the legacy. Legacies to the widow, children, and grandchildren of the deceased were exempt.[110] This tax went into effect on 1 July 1798 along with other tax-raising measures passed in anticipation of war with France. It was repealed on 1 July 1802.

Included in the tax package Congress passed in 1862 to help pay for the Civil War were stamp taxes on wills entered into probate and letters of administration issued and an inheritance tax on transfers of personal property.[111]

lineal issue, lineal ancestors, siblings	0.75%
descendants of siblings	1.5%
parents' siblings and their descendants	3.0%
grandparents' siblings and their descendants	4.0%
other relatives and unrelated individuals	5.0%

The inheritance tax was collected only if the value of the personal estate exceeded $1,000; bequests to the surviving spouse were exempt. Because the inheritance tax was based on kinship relationship, you may be able to determine the relationship of the specific heir to the deceased. For example, if the value of the personal estate were $6,000 and the tax collected $90 [$6,000 x 1.5% = $90], you have indirect evidence that the heir was a descendant of the decedent's sibling—in other words, the child of the deceased's brother or sister. Had the tax been lower, you could infer that the heir's relationship was closer based on the rate table above.

In 1864 the inheritance tax law was amended to increase the rates and to cover transfers of real estate. The stamp taxes and the inheritance tax were repealed in 1870, then revived again to help finance the Spanish-American War. The social reform movement of the late 1890s also favored an inheritance tax to curb the spectacular growth of inherited wealth.[112] In 1902 the inheritance tax was repealed along with most other taxes imposed to pay for the war. Another war, World War I, provided the impetuous for Congress to institute an estate tax that still exists today.[113]

The federal estate tax law passed in 1916 imposed a tax on the transfer of the net estate of every person dying after the passage of the law. The taxable net estate was determined by deducting funeral and administrative expenses, debts, losses, and a $50,000 exemption from the value of the gross estate. Initially, the tax rates ranged from one percent on the first $50,000 to ten percent on the amount over $5 million.[114] Changes in the law have modified both the tax rate schedule and the amount of the exemption as well as modifying the allowable deductions.

State Estate and Inheritance Taxes

Of more interest to genealogists are the inheritance taxes imposed by the states because the tax levied is based on the degree of kinship. Inheritance taxes are imposed on the right to inherit as opposed to the value of the estate. Those more closely related are deemed to have a greater right to inherit. The executor of the estate must determine the relationship to the deceased in order to prepare the tax return. Consequently, the relationship of the heirs to the deceased is usually stated on the tax return thus providing direct evidence of family relationships.

Most states began by taxing only collateral rather than direct beneficiaries (nephews and cousins, not wives and children, for example). Eventually all beneficiaries were taxed. Once a state began taxing all beneficiaries, it adjusted the tax rate or the exemption according to the beneficiary's relationship to the deceased: the closer the relationship, the lower the tax rate or the greater the exemption.

A word of caution: The meanings of collateral beneficiary and direct beneficiary varied by state and by time period. In 1901 Arkansas imposed an inheritance tax on collateral beneficiaries: everyone except the father, mother, husband, wife, lineal descendant, adopted child, and lineal descendants of an adopted child. In 1903 the definition of direct beneficiary was expanded to include the decedent's brother, sister, grandfather, and grandmother.[115]

Documents from a state that taxed only property left to collateral relatives, such as New Jersey's Record of Estates Subject to Collateral Inheritance Tax, required such information as:
- name of the deceased
- name of the beneficiary

- beneficiary's relationship to the decedent
- name of the executor or administrator
- date the will was entered into probate
- appraiser's return of estimated cash value
- ascertained cash value
- amount of tax due
- amount of the state treasurer's receipt
- date of receipt

The examples from New Jersey in Table 19 show how helpful an inheritance tax record can be in providing direct evidence of relationships.

**Table 19. Record of Estates Subject to
Collateral Inheritance Tax, New Jersey, 1912**

Testator or Intestate	Name of Person Subject to Tax	Relationship to Testator or Intestate
Josephine E. Cadmus	Henry Heath, Jr.	nephew
	Josephine Cadmus	niece of husband
	Walter Cadmus	son of stepson
	William G. Cadmus	son of stepson
	Maud McWilliams	daughter of stepson
	Josiah F. Cadmus MD	brother-in-law
	Harriet J. Cadmus	stepdaughter
	Josephine L.S. Heath	niece
William Trenwith	Mary Jane Barclay	children of Amelia E.
	Basil W. Hayes	Hayes, aunt of Wm.
	Robert E. Hayes	Trenwith
	Amelia Morris	
	Morris Trenwith Hayes	
	Annie MacFarlane	children of Julia
	John E. MacFarlane	MacFarlane, dec'd,
	Trenwith MacFarlane	daughter of Amelia E.
	G.H. MacFarlane	Hayes

Some states that taxed collateral relatives maintained records only for those estates that were subject to the inheritance tax, while other states kept records for every estate. In North Carolina, for example, if the only beneficiaries were direct relatives, the entry might read "estate of John Smith—widow and six children—no tax." New Hampshire, on the other hand, required that a report be filed with the state treasurer listing the names of all heirs-at-law and their relationship to the deceased as well as the legatees named in the will; the relationship of each to the deceased; and the age of each. This report was also to include those who predeceased the legator. Other states did not require such detailed information. In West Virginia, for example, you might find only a receipt for the total tax amount paid.

Pennsylvania first enacted an inheritance tax in 1826; Louisiana followed in 1828. Eighteen states had enacted inheritance tax laws by 1900, some for only brief periods of time. But by 1915—before the federal government enacted its own estate tax in 1916—almost all states had enacted some version of the inheritance tax. Appendix C lists effective dates for state inheritance tax laws through 1913. To supplement these laws, many states added a gift tax on transfers made during the donor's lifetime. These provisions were clearly intended to catch deathbed transfers made to avoid the inheritance tax. The federal gift tax was enacted in 1924 for the same reason.

After states became convinced that the federal estate tax would be in effect indefinitely, many began to impose a piggyback estate tax. Because the federal estate tax allowed a limited deduction for the amount of state inheritance or estate tax paid, many states decided that they might as well collect a portion of the tax instead of letting it all go to the federal government. The law in these states simply stated that the state tax would be equal to the maximum deduction allowed for state inheritance or estate taxes on the federal return. Consequently, by the end of the 20th century, most state inheritance tax returns provide little information beyond that on the federal return.

Research Example: Identify the Heirs of an Estate

The Colorado inheritance tax return filed for the estate of Irving S. Morse listed the property owned, its valuation, the expenditures made by the estate, the tax calculation, and the amount and type of distribution to each beneficiary. Some of this information duplicates information usually found in a probate file including the inventory of the estate and the accounting for disbursements. But the inheritance tax return may present the information in a different format, making some items stand out that otherwise might be overlooked.

The assets listed in the inheritance tax return for the Morse estate were organized by category: real estate, personal property, notes and mortgages. Most of the items are self-explanatory. There were a number of notes receivable (debts owed to the estate) that might provide additional family information. Might the borrower, for example, be a family member?

The inheritance tax return for the Irving S. Morse estate listed stock certificates for three different companies: Fox River Butter Company, Akron Oil and Gas, and Beatrice Creamery. Beatrice Creamery is of particular interest because it appears in several

**Table 20. Personal Property Listing
for Estate of Irving S. Morse**

Cert. 121 for 100 shares Fox River Butter Co.	$ -- 15,000.00
Cert. 34, for 400 shares Akron Oil & Gas Co.	no value
Cert. 18 for 200 shares Beatrice Creamery Co.	$ -- 33,000.00
Cert. 1407 for 75 shares Beatrice Creamery Co.	$ -- 12,375.00
Cert. 186 for 100 shares Beatrice Creamery Co.	$ --- 9,500.00
Cert. 183 for 200 shares Beatrice Creamery Co.	$ -- 19,100.00
Cert. 182 for 200 shares Beatrice Creamery Co.	$ -- 19,100.00
Bonds of the Kimball Irrigation District, @ $500 ea.	$ --- 7,000.00
One Cadillac Auto, Model 1913	$ ------700.00
Gold Watch	$ ------- 60.00

places in the list of assets including a large quantity of stock held, cash in the hands of the company, and a note receivable from the creamery. Clearly, learning more about this company might lead to additional information about Irving Morse.

In the Distribution of Estate each beneficiary was listed with his relationship to Morse and the value received. Not surprisingly, most of the estate went to the widow and two daughters. Other bequests went to Willis Brown, nephew; Otis Storrs, uncle; Edward Morse Brown, nephew; and Carrie Knight, cousin. Examining each of these individuals may provide additional family information.

A notation at the bottom of the third page indicated that Morse left a will. This document identified Sarah P. McConnell as Irving Morse's mother. There was also a bequest to Clara B. Snyder, an aunt, but no distribution to her, indicating that Clara probably had died between 7 July 1911, when the will was written, and 26 June 1916, when the inheritance tax return was filed.

Table 21. Distribution of Estate of Irving S. Morse

Total amount of decedent's real estate - - - - - - - - - - - - - - - $			9,400.00
Total amount of decedent's personal estate - - - - - - - - - - - - $			134,632.11
Total - $			144.032.11
From which debts, expenses are to be deducted, amounting to - - $			12,236.11
Leaving the sum of - - - - - - - - - - - - - - - - - $			131,796.00

which is the net estate transferred from decedent, and is divided as follows:

Hattie E. Morse	Wife	Absolute - $	90,957.25
Clara Morse Winner	Dtr.	Absolute - $	14,919.37
Mary Morse	Dtr.	Absolute - $	14,919.38
Willis Brown	Neph.	Absolute - $	4,498.33
Otis Storrs	Uncle	Life --- $	1,204.00
Edw. Morse Brown	Neph.	Absolute - $	4,498.33
Carrie Knight	Cousin	Absolute - $	799.34
Total amount of property transferred - - - - - - - - - - - - - - - $			131,796.00

Based on this information, you can form some hypotheses:

- Irving and Hattie Morse had only two daughters living in 1911.
- Irving's mother, Sarah, must have remarried some time after the birth of Irving Morse, since her surname was McConnell, not Morse.
- Nephews Willis Brown and Edward Morse Brown are probably the children of Irving's sister, who perhaps had died before 1911 since she is not mentioned in the will.
- Otis Storrs is possibly Irving's mother's brother.
- Carrie Knight may be the married daughter of either Otis Storrs or Clara Snyder, since they each received bequests.

Additional research using other documents including birth and death certificates (if they exist), marriage records, and additional probate court records could clarify each of these relationships.

Probate files may include copies of the inheritance tax returns and receipts for taxes paid. The governmental entity that collected the tax should also have a copy. Even though the tax was mandated by the state, it might have been collected by the county and turned over to the state. Of course, some records have been lost, some destroyed, and some turned over to an archive.

Estate and Inheritance Taxes Can Prove Relationships

Estate and inheritance taxes are assessed only once and therefore lack the comparative data that make other tax records so useful. The fact that these records are comparatively recent also limits their usefulness primarily to searches in the late 19th and early 20th centuries. But where they do exist, they provide direct or indirect evidence of relationships.

---

[110] *U.S. Stats at Large*, 1:536.

[111] *U.S. Stats at Large*, 12:483.

[112] Sidney Ratner, *American Taxation: Its History as a Social Force in Democracy* (New York: W.W. Norton & Company, Inc., 1942), 353.

[113] Ibid., 354.

[114] Ibid., 356-57.

[115] Arthur W. Blakemore and High Bancroft, *The Inheritance Law, Containing All American Decisions and Existing Statutes, with Supplement, Inheritance Taxes in 1912 and 1913* (Boston: Boston Book Company, 1914), 307.

Chapter 8. Miscellaneous Tax Records

You can have a lord, you can have a king, but the man to fear is the tax collector.

Sumerian proverb

Taxes take many forms and may have been paid with money, commodities, or personal labor. During the American colonial period service to the community was required of male citizens. Militia duty, road construction and maintenance, service as jail guards and constables were all forms of taxation through public service. Those who failed to attend to their assigned duties were fined.

Militia Service

Militia duty was the earliest community service in the American colonies. The Virginia militia formed the only defense against Indian attacks and was organized as early as 1623 when the governor authorized a levy of "forty able and sufficient men" from all the plantations. Men who had arrived in Virginia before 1612 were excused and "such persons as remain at home" were directed to work the ground of those serving in the militia who were "abroad upon the march."[116]

As communities grew, every free white man between the ages of 16 and 50 was required to render military service and to answer the muster call several times each year. Those who did not were fined. The General Assembly of Virginia directed that militia officers fine delinquents 100 pounds of tobacco for each unexcused absence.[117] Lists of those who were fined can sometimes be found in court minute books.

Militia members were usually the same as the male taxpayers. Tax ledgers frequently included lists of the members of militia units with their captains. Virginia militia rolls routinely give the soldier's place of birth, age, residence, occupation, and physical description.[118] The enlisting officer sometimes made these lists even more informative by recording his personal impression of the soldier.

Although New England colonists kept their muskets handy from the earliest period of settlement, the first militia units in Massachusetts Bay Colony were organized in 1636. The colony required all males between the ages of 16 and 45 to possess arms and defend the community.[119]

The U.S. Constitution, ratified in 1787, provided for a militia. Subsequently, Congress passed the Militia Act in 1792, which required that all able-bodied white male citizens aged 18 to 45 be enrolled in a general militia. Citizen soldiers were also required to provide themselves with a firearm and ammunition, a knapsack, and supplies.[120]

In Georgia and Tennessee militia districts were the same as the tax districts. These militia districts were originally laid out to include the number of available males best suited to the operation of a military company. The elected militia captain created the tax list and also served as the tax collector. Tax districts were designated by the current militia captain's name. The name changed each year although the individuals within a district remained more or less the same from year to year.

Western territories used militia troops in their continuing struggles with Native Americans. In 1850 California enacted its first military law, which was patterned after the federal Militia Act of 1792. The first San Francisco militia company was established in 1849 and named itself the First California Guard. To finance itself the unit formed a joint stock company whose members subscribed to 300 shares of stock at $100 per share. The funds enabled this organization to construct a lavish Military Hall and armory.[121] Local newspapers of the period included lists of members of the militia organizations and their activities.

In 1863 Colorado Territorial Legislature enacted a law establishing a militia funded by a military poll tax. The tax money was used to buy some uniforms and other supplies, but it was never enough to pay for guns and ammunition. The tax also seems to have been irregularly collected. Several militia groups in Colorado collected dues to supplement the funds for the organization. [122]

Colorado Military Poll Tax

Each male inhabitant of Bent County, Colorado, of the age of 21 years and upwards is subject to pay a Military Poll Tax of fifty cents for the year 1872 by order of the Territorial Auditor.

May 9, 1873

R.M. McMurray, Treasurer

Figure 13. Notice of military poll tax, published 27 June 1873 in the Las Animas Leader, Colorado Territory, 1873.

Some Colorado counties added a column for the military poll tax to their real estate tax books. Other counties created separate lists for the tax. A surviving military poll tax list for 1899 Arapahoe County, Colorado (part of which became Denver County in 1901) is a neatly alphabetized list of the names and addresses of each adult male who paid the one-dollar tax. The list is from the period of the Spanish-American War and seems to represent a high point in military patriotism. During World War I, a similar outpouring of patriotism pushed collections up. This tax was discontinued in 1919.

From the first establishment of the colonies, through the American Revolution, the War of 1812, the Seminole War in Florida in the mid-1830s, and the Mexican War in 1845, the Civil War, and the Spanish American War, militia units have fought in every military engagement in U.S. history. The formation of the National Guard early in the 1900s assumed many militia duties, but various state militias continue to exist as State Defense Forces.

Road Orders

As families moved into the interior of the country, people needed to travel between their homes and the courthouse, the church, the store, and the public house. Paths between major landmarks became roads. Eventually, these roads were linked together to form major migration trails. No county services to build or maintain roads existed, making local residents responsible for maintaining their own portion of the road. If a resident wanted a road constructed, he petitioned the court, which appointed representatives to determine whether the proposed road was needed and, if so, where it should be constructed. Once the best route for the new road was determined, the court issued a road order directing the residents along that portion of the road to keep the path cleared and maintained.

Road supervisors were appointed by the court, and the heads of households were ordered to contribute workers to the road program. Those who failed to contribute to road maintenance were fined by the court. By studying the road orders for colonial Virginia (many of which have been published), it is possible to determine the route of the proposed road, learn whether your ancestor lived along the proposed road, and who his neighbors were.

> **Road Order**
> *Entered by the Amelia County, Virginia, Court, July 1771:*
> The laboring tithables of Peter Claybrook, John Harris, William Rucker, John Claybrook, Mordecai Rucker, Parroll Prindle, Joel Meadors, Elisha Rucker, Stephen Johnson, William Winston, and Judith Bentley ordered to clean and repair the road.

Figure 14. Road Order, Amelia County, Virginia, 1771.

The practice of contributing labor as a form of tax did not end with the colonial period. The Oklahoma Territorial Assembly passed a general property tax law to finance the construction of public roads after severe flooding in 1902 made travel virtually impossible. The funding from the general property tax was inadequate so the legislature enacted a road tax. This law included the requirement that all men between the ages of 21 and 45 donate four eight-hour days a year to work on the highways. Those who refused to work were fined $5 for each absence. Records are generally not available, although there may be some in historical or genealogical repositories in individual counties.[123]

Ecclesiastical Taxes

In many areas of colonial America churches were supported by public tax money. The Church of England became the established church in Virginia in 1609; in Massachusetts in 1630 (until the Congregational Church became the established church in 1660); in New Jersey before 1660; in the lower part of New York in 1693; in Maryland in 1702; in South Carolina in 1706; in North Carolina in 1730; and in Georgia in 1758. Local taxes were used to pay ministers and erect churches, support the poor, care for the sick and infirm, supply food to the elderly and impoverished, and bury paupers.

In 1660 Massachusetts colonists established the Congregational Church as the official church, supported by taxes. After the American Revolution, Massachusetts approved a new state constitution that included a "general assessment tax for religion," which continued tax support for religion but allowed each taxpayer to designate which church his share would support. Similar language was included in the new constitutions of Connecticut and New Hampshire. In 1791 Connecticut required dissenters to file certificates of dissent and statements of membership in a dissenting Church in order to be exempt from the state tithe. Maryland and Georgia also passed general assessment laws for religion, but they were not implemented.[124] Taxes levied to support churches were eventually repealed in 1818 in Connecticut and in 1833 in Massachusetts after lengthy legal and legislative battles.[125]

As the result of political maneuvering, Virginia abolished the established Church of England at the end of the Revolutionary

War and did not continue state funding for churches. In 1789 the state created the civil position of "overseer of the poor" to monitor the care of the indigent replacing services formerly provided by the church. Pennsylvania never levied a tax for any religion because Quakers opposed the establishment of any official church.

Faculty Taxes

The faculty tax was a form of income tax used in an attempt to tax each man on his ability to earn: "All men shall be rated in all rates for their whole abilitie, wheresoever it lyes."[126] Colonies that had urban populations such as Massachusetts, Connecticut, Pennsylvania, and New York, enacted faculty taxes on skilled laborers who were rated or taxed according to their income gains just as other men were taxed on the probable income of their land. Merchants were also taxed on their transactions and their stock on hand. Attorneys and physicians as well as those who loaned out money were also assessed faculty taxes. This early form of income tax was meant to include all men in the support of the local government "each according to his abilities," but it was never a major source of tax revenue.

Business Licenses

Licenses have been required in order to operate certain types of businesses almost from the beginning of organized county and town government in the American colonies. People who wanted to operate a tavern or ferry were required to purchase a license. As communities and businesses grew, so too did the requirements for licensing. Ohio, as early as 1792, required licenses for sellers of whiskey and other spirits, merchants, taverns, auctioneers, ferry operators, and peddlers of merchandise made outside the U.S.

Ohio also required that a tavern have at least four rooms, three fireplaces and a stable with six stalls for horses.[127] Tax books frequently include lists of people who had paid the annual license fee for the year, and court order books report the establishment of requirements for these licenses.

Liquor Taxes

From earliest colonial times the public house or "ordinary" was required to be licensed. County governments also routinely established the legal prices to be charged for each type of beverage. Operators who tried to sell liquor without a license were fined.

Farmers in western Pennsylvania, Maryland, Virginia, and North Carolina used liquor as a form of money just as Virginians had used tobacco. After the Revolutionary War the federal government passed a liquor excise tax on spirits distilled from grain adopting Alexander Hamilton's view that liquor was a luxury item. The resulting Whiskey Rebellion was swiftly put down, and the leaders eventually given amnesty, but the tax remained.

Distilled liquor continued to be a major source of tax revenue for the federal government. From 1868 until 1913 taxes on distilled liquor represented 90 percent of all internal revenue collections.[128] After 1933, in the wake of the repeal of Prohibition, governments found that liquor remained an easy target of taxation.

School Taxes

Massachusetts and Connecticut towns imposed taxes as early as the 1650s to support public education. By 1811 Pennsylvania primary education was funded by taxes, and Pennsylvania tax assessors began recording the names of parents, children, and teachers in the tax records.[129]

The movement to fund public education, however, grew in the 1840s as thousands of immigrants poured in and overwhelmed the social systems of port cities.[130] Northeastern states began enacting taxes to support public or "poor" schools, and the public education movement spread quickly to the Midwest. Tax records frequently record the number of school-aged children and the names of their parents.

Federal Head Tax on Aliens

Immigration records may also include tax records. In the Immigration Act of 3 August 1882, Congress imposed a head tax of 50 cents on each immigrant. Initially transportation companies paid this tax on each passenger who arrived by sea. In order to collect the head tax from immigrants entering the U.S. by land, the government began issuing Alien Certificates to those immigrants coming across contiguous land borders. These certificates served as entry permits.

Alien certificates were handwritten on preprinted government forms and included the immigrant's name and nationality; a physical description; the place where the immigrant entered the U.S.; and the date the certificate was surrendered to an immigration official. Certificates for non-Canadian citizens

Fig. 15. Federal Alien Certificate for Gustaf A. Dahlin." Certificates of Head Tax Paid by Aliens Arriving at Seattle from Foreign Contiguous Territory, 1917-1924." M1365, roll 1, (Washington, D.C.: National Archives).

arriving at Seattle, Washington, included information about the date, vessel and port of arrival into Canada. The National Archives has microfilmed certificates of individuals arriving at Seattle between 1917 and 1924 in microfilm publication M1365 (10 rolls) arranged by date of arrival. Additionally, manifests such as those included in the St. Albans, Vermont, records of immigration from Canada to the United States include a box for reporting head tax status.

Old Age Assistance Tax

Early in the 20th century some states started to move away from the concept of the poor farm, believing that it would be less expensive to pay poor individuals to live on their own instead of having the local government support a poor farm or poor house.

The applications for old age assistance are of special interest to genealogists because they often contain a great deal of personal information including date and place of birth, physical condition, and names and addresses of relatives. In order to finance old age assistance, the states allowed counties to impose a tax that went into a separate fund. The tax was usually collected along with property taxes and, in fact, was sometimes a surcharge to those property taxes.

Arizona in 1915 was the first state to pass a law providing for the collection and distribution of old age assistance. This early law was declared unconstitutional by the Arizona State Supreme Court but was revived in 1933. Other states followed, and by 1934 28 states and two territories had passed old age assistance laws. Some states passed laws making it optional for counties to assess additional tax and provide assistance, but most states made it mandatory. Eligibility requirements varied by state; in those states where these programs were voluntary, requirements could vary by county:

- Most states (except Arizona and Hawaii) refused to make payments to older people who had children or relatives who could support them.
- Most required the recipient to be a U.S. citizen and resident of the state for at least 15 years.
- Many required the recipient to transfer any property he possessed to the pension authority before receiving any payment.
- Most had property and income caps to limit eligibility.

- Most denied benefits to anyone who gave away property in order to qualify for public assistance.
- Most required that a lien be placed on the estate of the recipient to be collected upon his death.
- Most denied benefits to anyone who had deserted a spouse, failed to support his family, committed any crime, or had been a tramp or beggar.
- Benefits were denied to inmates of jails, prisons, infirmaries, and insane asylums; a few permitted the payment of assistance for inmates of a benevolent fraternal institution.

With requirements such as these, the application form clearly provided the government (and now genealogists and historians) with a great deal of information about the applicant. By 1934 the percentage of the eligible population enrolled in these programs was quite small, ranging from 0.2 percent in Maryland (141 out of 92,972) to 21.6 percent in Arizona (1,974 out of 9,118), no doubt due to stringent eligibility requirements. The application records, however, may provide you with important personal information and are worth researching. With the advent of Social Security in 1937, these laws were gradually repealed. Appendix D provides information on the various state old age assistance laws in effect by 1934.

Once you have determined whether the state you are interested in distributed old age assistance payments, you will need to locate the records. Since the assistance was generally provided at the county level, the records were originally maintained there. Some counties have turned their records over to the state archives, and some still have the records in the local courthouse. Iowa researchers have long been familiar with the applications for assistance under its old age assistance tax. Those records have been microfilmed and are available at the Iowa State Archives and at the Family History Library in Salt Lake City. In Colorado, on the other hand, some counties turned their records over to the Colorado State Archives in Denver, while others, such as Archuleta County, gave those records to the county historical society, which extracted them and put them online.[131] Unfortunately, not all records survive.

[116] William L. Shea, *The Virginia Militia in the Seventeenth Century* (Baton Rouge, Louisiana: Louisiana State University Press, 1983), 40-41.
[117] Ibid., 75.
[118] See examples of these descriptions in *Virginia's Colonial Soldiers* by Lloyd DeWitt Bockstruck (Baltimore: Genealogical Publishing Co., Inc., 1988), 73.
[119] Douglas, *Financial History of Massachusetts*, Vol. 1, No. 4, 69.
[120] *Militia Act of 1792*, Second Congress, Session I, Chap. VIII, 8 May 1792.
[121] Col. Norman S. Marshall and CWO2 Mark J. Denger, "The Creation of the National Guard of California," at http://www.militarymuseum.org/CreationNGC.html : accessed 28 July 2006.
[122] Maj. John H. Nankivell, *History of the Military Organizations of the State of Colorado, 1860-1935* (Denver, Colorado, W. H. Kistler Stationery Co., 1935), 75.
[123] Alice Eichholz, editor, *Ancestry's Redbook: American State, County and Town Sources,* Revised Edition (Salt Lake City, Utah: Ancestry, 1992), 594.
[124] "Religion and the Founding of the American Republic," Library of Congress on-line pamphlet, http://www.loc.gov/exhibits/religion/re105.html : accessed 7 March 2006.
[125] Sanford Cobb, *The Rise of Religious Liberty in America: A History* (New York: MacMillan, 1902), Chapter X.
[126] *Massachusetts Records*, I:82.
[127] "Ohio Taxes Through Time," http://tax.ohio.gov/documents/publications/2003_Annual_Report/Ohio%20Taxes%20Through%20Time.pdf : accessed 27 May 2006.
[128] Doris, *The American Way in Taxation: Internal Revenue, 1862-1963,* 19.
[129] "Enumeration of School Children, 1811-1816," microfilm, Philadelphia City Archives, 3101 Market Street, Philadelphia, Pennsylvania 19104.
[130] Carl F. Kaestle, Introduction, *School, The Story of American Public Education* by Sheila Curran Bernard and Sarah Mondale (Boston: Beacon Press, 2001), iv.

[131] Archuleta County, Colorado, old age assistance records, http://www.rootsweb.com/~coarchul/oldage.htm : accessed 16 December 2005.

Chapter 9. Summary

Taxes are the price we pay for civilization.

Justice Oliver Wendell Holmes

There are no simple rules for researching tax records. The definition of who was taxable, what property was taxable, what rate was applied to which property, and who was doing the taxing all influence tax records. The records themselves can vary from a simple list of people who paid a one-time tax to finance a single project to a complex personal property tax form with 60 or more taxable categories. In addition, the record-keeping methods and the tax districts often changed from one year to the next.

There are, however, similarities. Generally speaking, only adult males were taxable. The tax lists were frequently arranged in rough alphabetical order by surname within each tax district. The tax lists generally provided some identifying information to distinguish between men in the community with the same surname. Finally, the property being taxed was identified and sometimes described. Additionally, tax records often included bits of information not available in other records. These may include occupation, marital status, type of dwelling, number and sometimes names of school children.

By studying the many ways Americans have been taxed throughout the past 400 years, genealogists can learn the effects of taxation on family history, family movement, and family wealth. The benefits to research in tax records are numerous. You will find information that will enable you to:

- Locate an ancestor in a specific county and state at a specific time period.
- Track an ancestor's movement from one location to another.
- Narrow the date range for establishing residence in a specific location by determining first and last year of taxation.
- Confirm land ownership, acres owned and even location.
- Gather information about a landless ancestor.
- Separate men with the same name in the same county.
- Identify men as they reach adulthood and are taxed in their own right.
- Establish an ancestor's year of death as his estate appears in the tax rolls.
- Estimate the wealth of an ancestor based on his taxable property.
- Use the information found in tax records to lead to other valuable records.

Summary of Research Techniques

Learn and practice the research techniques described below to become more effective in your research of tax records.

- Search for tax records, usually at the county level, for the correct time period.
- Learn what the column headings are in all tax records to determine what information was being collected.

- Consider the many spelling variations for the surnames of your ancestors.

After you have located an ancestor in the tax records:

- Do a year-by-year comparison of tax records, if available.
- Calculate the amount of tax.
- Look for collateral relatives in the same tax records.
- Write a formal hypothesis.
- Develop a preliminary research plan.

As you study tax records you will need to develop specific skills to decipher old handwriting, recognize common abbreviations, and calculate tax amounts in pounds, shillings, and pence to enhance your understanding of the information presented.

There is much to be gained from researching tax records. We hope we have provided you with the tools to begin your research into tax records whether you use these records as a simple census, as a way to identify male ancestors, or to gather specific information about the life of your ancestor. Let this book inspire you to explore those records.

Appendix A
Textural Records of the Direct Tax Commission in the Southern States, National Archives Record Group 58.4

ALABAMA

Applications to redeem land sold for taxes	1880-1889
Claims	1870-1880
Commission reports	1864-1867

ARKANSAS

Applications to redeem land sold for taxes	1870-1887
Letters received	1864-1867

FLORIDA

Applications to redeem land sold for taxes	1864-1887
Claims	1875-1887
Commission reports	1864-1867; 1873
Letters received	1864-1882
Letters sent	1865-1867
Lists of land sold	1864-1882
Tax sale certificates	1864-1866

GEORGIA

Letters received	1865-1867
Letters sent	1865-1867

LOUISIANA

Letters received	1864-1867
Records of sales of cotton	1860-1866

MISSISSIPPI

Records of sales of cotton	1866
Records of products shipped from Vicksburg	1865-1867

NORTH CAROLINA
Letters received   1864-1866

SOUTH CAROLINA
Preliminary Inventory of the Records of the United States Direct Tax
Commission for the District of South Carolina by Jane Greene.
Preliminary Index No. 14, Washington: 1948.

Applications for refunds of surplus proceeds of property sold for taxes	1891-1898
Applications to make final redemption payments	1872-1875
Applications to redeem land sold for taxes	1872-1899
Certifications of land sold for taxes	1863-1886
General correspondence	1862-1893
Land certificates issued to heads of families of African race	1863-1872
Maps of St. Helena's and St. Luke's Parishes, Beaufort County	1855, 1864-1895
Maps of Port Royal	1913, 1920
Minutes of the commission	1862-1870
Registers of applications to redeem property and make final payments	1872-1874
Registers of certificates of release	1872-1875
Registers of claims	1871-1899
Registers of tax sale certificates	1863-1878
Survey field notebooks, Hilton Head and other coastal islands	1863-1868
Tax sale certificates	1863-1866

TENNESSEE
Microform publication T227, Civil War Direct Tax Assessment Lists:
    Tennessee, 6 rolls

Applications for refunds of surplus proceeds of property sold for taxes	1864-1884
Applications to redeem land sold for taxes	1864-1874
Letters received	1864-1874
Proceedings of the commission	1863-1866
Tax sale certificates	1864-1866

TEXAS

Claims	1865-1873
Commission reports	1865-1867
Minutes of the commission	1865-1866
Receipts for direct taxes	1866-1868

VIRGINIA

Applications to redeem land sold for taxes	1864-1884
Commission reports	1864-1866
Cotton returns	1862-1868, 1903
Letters received	1863-1882
Minutes of the commission	1863-1866
Tax certificates	1864-1866

Appendix B
Microfilmed Records of the Internal Revenue Assessment Lists, 1862-1874, National Archives Record Group 58

M754	Alabama, 1865-1866, 6 rolls
M755	Arkansas, 1865-1866, 2 rolls
T1208	Arkansas, 1867-1874, 4 rolls
M756	California, 1862-1866, 33 rolls
M757	Colorado, 1862-1866, 3 rolls
M758	Connecticut, 1862-1866, 23 rolls
M759	Delaware, 1862-1866, 8 rolls
M760	District of Columbia, 1862-1866, 8 rolls
M761	Florida, 1865-1866, 1 roll
M762	Georgia, 1865-1866, 8 rolls
M763	Idaho, 1865-1866, 1 roll
T1209	Idaho, 1867-1874, 1 roll
M764	Illinois, 1862-1866, 63 rolls
M765	Indiana, 1862-1866, 42 rolls
M766	Iowa, 1862-1866, 16 rolls
M767	Kansas, 1862-1866, 3 rolls
M768	Kentucky, 1862-1866, 24 rolls
M769	Louisiana, 1863-1866, 10 rolls
M770	Maine, 1862-1866, 15 rolls
M771	Maryland, 1862-1866, 21 rolls
M773	Michigan, 1862-1866, 15 rolls
M774	Minnesota, 1862-1866, 3 rolls
M775	Mississippi, 1865-1866, 3 rolls
M776	Missouri, 1862-1865, 22 rolls
M777	Montana, 1864-1872, 1 roll
M779	Nevada, 1863-1866, 2 rolls
M780	New Hampshire, 1862-1866, 10 rolls

M782	New Mexico, 1862-1870, 1872-1874, 1 roll
M603	New York and New Jersey, 1862-1866, 218 rolls
M784	North Carolina, 1864-1866, 2 rolls
M1631	Oregon, 1867-1873, 2 rolls
M787	Pennsylvania, 1862-1866, 107 rolls
M788	Rhode Island, 1862-1866, 10 rolls
M789	South Carolina, 1864-1866, 2 rolls
M791	Texas, 1865-1866, 2 rolls
M792	Vermont, 1862-1866, 7 rolls
M793	Virginia, 1862-1866, 6 rolls
M795	West Virginia, 1862-1866, 4 rolls

Appendix C
State Inheritance Tax Laws Through 1913

State	Years	Comments
Alabama	1848-1868	
Alaska	none	
Arizona	1912–	
Arkansas	1901–	
California	1853-1854; 1893–	initial tax on nonresidents only
Colorado	1901–	
Connecticut	1889–	
Delaware	1869–	
Florida	none	
Georgia	1913–	
Hawaii	1892–	
Idaho	1907–	
Illinois	1895–	
Indiana	1913–	
Iowa	1896–	
Kansas	1909–1913	
Kentucky	1906–	
Louisiana	1828-1830; 1842-1877; 1894; 1904–	initially on nonresident aliens only; 1894 tax ruled unconstitutional
Maine	1893–	
Maryland	1844–	
Massachusetts	1841-1891; 1891–	probate fee from 1841-1891
Michigan	1893; 1899–	1893 tax ruled unconstitutional
Minnesota	1875–	various laws ruled unconstitutional
Mississippi	none	
Missouri	1895–	
Montana	1897–	
Nebraska	1901–	
Nevada	1913–	

State	Years	Comments
New Hampshire	1878-1883; 1905–	initial law ruled unconstitutional
New Jersey	1892–	
New Mexico	none	
New York	1885–	
North Carolina	1847-1874; 1897–	
North Dakota	1903–	
Ohio	1893–	
Oklahoma	1907–	
Oregon	1903–	
Pennsylvania	1826–	
Rhode Island	none	
South Carolina	none	
South Dakota	1905–	
Tennessee	1891–	
Texas	1907–	
Utah	1901–	
Vermont	1862–	probate fees
Virginia	1843–	
Washington	1901–	
Washington D C	none	
West Virginia	1887–	
Wisconsin	1868–	sliding scale of probate fees
Wyoming	1903–	

Appendix D
State Old Age Assistance Laws, as of 1934

State or Territory	Year Law Enacted	Type of Law Mandatory or Optional	No. of Pensioners	Number of Persons of Eligible Age	Average Pension
Alaska	1913	M	446	3,437	$20.82
Arizona	1933	M	1,974	9,118	9.01
California	1929	M	19,300	210,379	21.16
Colorado	1927	M	8,705	61,787	8.59
Delaware	1931	M	1,610	16,678	9.79
Hawaii	1931	O	No information available		
Idaho	1931	M	1,275	22,310	8.85
Indiana	1933	M	23,418	138,426	6.13
Iowa	1934	M	3,000	184,239	13.50
Kentucky	1926	O	No pensions being paid		
Maine	1933	M	Not yet in effect		
Maryland	1927	O	141	92,972	29.90
Massachusetts	1930	M	20,023	156,590	24.35
Michigan	1933	M	2,660	148,853	9.59
Minnesota	1929	O	2,655	94,401	13.20
Montana	1923	O	1,781	14,377	7.28
Nebraska	1933	M	No action due to lack of funds		
Nevada	1925	O	23	4,814	15.00
New Hampshire	1931	M	1,423	25,714	19.06
New Jersey	1931	M	10,560	112,594	12.72
New York	1930	M	51,228	373,878	22.16
North Dakota	1933	M	No pensions being paid		
Ohio	1931	M	24,000	414,836	13.99
Oregon	1931	M	County ; no statewide data available.		
Pennsylvania	1934	M	Law just put into effect; no data available		
Utah	1929	M	930	22,665	8.56
Washington	1931	M	2,239	101,503	N/A
West Virginia	1931	O	No pensions being paid		
Wisconsin	1925	O	1,969	112,112	16.75
Wyoming	1929	M	643	8,707	10.79

Source: "Old Age Security Staff Report," by Barbara Nachtried Armstrong and Staff, 1934, from unpublished studies by the staff of the Committee on Economic Security (CES), Volume II, at www.ssa.gov/history/reports/ces/ces2armstaff.html (accessed 3/19/2005).

Glossary

administrator: person appointed by the court to administer the
   estate of a deceased person.

ad valorem tax: a tax based on value rather than on a flat rate; also
   a duty or charge laid upon goods, at a certain rate per cent
   upon their value, as stated in their invoice.

agent: person acting for another individual.

capitation tax: any tax imposed on a per capita basis. See *head tax*;
   poll tax.

defaulter: an individual who did not pay his taxes for one reason
   or another; usually listed in the back of the tax record account
   for that year.

estate tax: tax levied on the net estate of the deceased after
   allowable deductions for funeral expenses, administrative
   costs, debts, losses, and a set standard exemption.

excise tax: an internal tax levied on the manufacture, sale, or
   consumption of a commodity.

executor/executrix: individual named in a will or appointed by a
   court to executor the directions of the testor.

faculty tax: generally a tax applied to the estimated income of
   artisans such as silversmiths and glassblowers and
   professionals such as attorneys, and physicians.

headrights: right to claim a fixed amount of land as a reward for
   paying for the transportation of individuals into the new
   settlement area.

head tax: any tax imposed on a per capita basis.

import duties: tax levied on goods brought into the country from
   another country.

inheritance tax: tax levied on the right to inherit property. See
   legacy tax, succession tax.

land tax: tax levied on real estate owned, based on amount of land, location, and sometimes quality of the land.

legacy tax: tax on the right to inherit personal property. See *inheritance tax, succession tax.*

memorial: description of the history of ownership for a particular parcel of land, sometimes included in the tax record.

personal property tax: tax levied on tangible property other than land and its appurtenances. May include a wide variety of property including vehicles, livestock, gold, silver, stocks and bonds, musical instruments, furniture, jewelry.

poll tax: a fixed tax levied on each taxable individual. Also referred to as a head tax or a capitation tax; sometimes used for voting qualification.

probate fee: a fee imposed when an estate is settled by the court; either a flat rate or a graduated rate so that larger estates pay higher fees.

quitrent: an annual payment of a fixed rate of several shillings for each hundred acres of land, secured a freeman's title to his land; it was paid in lieu of the services traditionally required by feudal custom.

rate: to assess or set a value for the purposes of taxation.

rate list: annual list of all taxable property in the district.

succession tax: tax on the right to inherit personal property. See *inheritance tax, legacy tax.*

tariff: a schedule of tax duties imposed by a government on imported or exported goods.

tax farmer: independent contractor who collects taxes for the governmental entity in return for a percentage of the taxes collected.

tithable: taxable individual; also the person or property subject to tax.

tithe: land tax levied in New Netherlands (later New York) amounting to one-tenth of the annual harvest

Research Bibliography

Adams, Charles. *For Good and Evil: The Impact of Taxes on the Course of Civilization*. Lanham, Maryland: Madison Books, 1999.

------. *Those Dirty Rotten Taxes: The Tax Revolts That Built America*. New York: The Free Press, 1998.

Adams, Henry Carter. *Taxation in the United States, 1789-1816*. New York: Johnson Reprint Corp., 1973.

American State Papers: Finance, Washington: Gales and Seaton, 1832-1861.

Beers, Henry Putney. *The Confederacy: A Guide to the Archives of the Government of the Confederate States of America*. Washington, D.C.: National Archives and Records Administration, 1986.

Bernard, Sheila Curran and Sarah Mondale. *School, The Story of American Public Education*, with an Introduction by Carl F. Kaestle. Boston: Beacon Press, 2001.

Blakemore, Arthur W. and Hugh Bancroft. *The Inheritance Tax Law, Containing All American Decisions and Existing Statutes, with Supplement, Inheritance Taxes in 1912 and 1913*. Boston: Boston Book Company, 1914.

Bockstruck, Lloyd D. *Virginia's Colonial Soldiers*. Baltimore: Genealogical Publishing Co., 1988.

Brownlee, W. Elliot, *Federal Taxation in America: A Short History*, second edition, Washington D. C.: Woodrow Wilson Center Press and Cambridge University Press, 2004.

Cobb, Sanford. *The Rise of Religious Liberty in America: A History*. New York: MacMillan, 1902.

Cox, Cathy, Georgia Secretary of State. "Georgia Tax Records FAQ." http://www.sos.state.ga.us/archives/rs/taxfaq.htm : accessed 1 April 2001.

Dewey, Davis Rich, *Financial History of the United States*, New York: Longmans, Green and Co., 1928.

Doris, Lillian, editor. *The American Way in Taxation: Internal Revenue, 1862-1963*. Englewood Cliffs, New Jersey: Prentice-Hall, Inc., 1963.

Douglas, Charles H. J., *The Financial History of Massachusetts From the Organization of the Massachusetts Bay Company to the American*

Revolution, Studies in History, Economics and Public Law, Vol. 1, No. 4. New York: AMS Press, 1892.

Dowell, Stephen. *A History of Taxation and Taxes in England*, vol. 2. London: 1965, reprint of 1884 edition.

Eakle, Arlene Haslam. *Tax Records: A Common Source with An Uncommon Value*. No Location: A. H. Eakle, 1978.

Edwards, Conley L., Virginia State Archivist. "Using Land Tax Records in the Archives at the Library of Virginia," Research Notes No. 1. Revised 1999. http://www.lva.lib.va.us/whatwehave/ land/rn1_landtax.html/

Eichholz, Alice, editor. *Red Book: American State, County, and Town Sources*. 3rd ed. Provo, Utah: Ancestry, 2004.

Einhorn, Robin L. *American Taxation, American Slavery*. Chicago: University of Chicago Press, 2006.

Everton, George B. *The Handybook for Genealogists: United States of America*. Draper, Utah: Everton Publishers, 2002.

Forsythe, Dall W. Taxation and Political Change in the Young Nation, 1781-1833. New York: Columbia University Press, 1977.

Gentry, Daphne. "Headrights," Research Notes No. 4, Library of Virginia online at www.lva.lib.va.us/whatwehave/local/ va4_headrights.htm.

Gentry, Daphne. "Taxes in Colonial Virginia," Research Notes No. 20, Library of Virginia online at www.lva.lib.va.us/whatwehave/ local/va20_coltax.htm.

Giroux, Gary and Johns, Sharon, "Financing the Civil War: The Office of Internal Revenue and the Use of Revenue Stamps," http://acct.tamu.edu/giroux/fininacingcivil.htm : accessed 5 December 2005.

Heinegg, Paul. *Free African Americans of North Carolina and Virginia*. Baltimore, Maryland: Clearfield Co., Inc., 1997.

Hening, William Waller. *The Statutes at Large Being a Collection of All the Laws of Virginia from the First Session of the Legislature, in the Year 1619*, 13 vols. Richmond, New York, and Philadelphia, 1819-1823; Reprint, Charlottesville, Virginia: University Press of Virginia, 1969.

Jensen, Jens Peter, *Property Taxation in The United States*. Chicago: University of Chicago Press, 1931

Jones, Frederick Robertson. *History of Taxation in Connecticut, 1636-1776*. Johns Hopkins University Studies in Historical and Political Science,

Fourteenth Series, No. 8, August 1896. Baltimore: Johns Hopkins Press.

Kinsman, Delos O., *The Income Tax in the Commonwealths of the United States*, Publications of the American Economic Association, Vol. IV, No. 4, New York: Macmillan Company, 1908.

Kolbe, J. Christian. "Colonial Tithables," Research Notes No. 17, Library of Virginia website, www.lva.lib.va.us/whatwehave/tax/rn17_tithables.htm.

Library of Congress, "Religion and the Founding of the American Republic," http://www.loc.gov/exhibits/religion/rel05.html : accessed 7 March 2006.

Library of Virginia. "Colonial Tithables," Research Notes No. 17. http://www.lva.lib.va.us/whatwehave/tax/rn17_tithables.htm : accessed 12 July 2004.

Luebking, Sandra Hargreaves. "Research in Land and Tax Records," *The Source: A Guidebook of American Genealogy*, rev. ed., Loretto Dennis Szucs and Sandra Hargreaves Luebking, editors. Salt Lake City, Utah: 1997.

Marshall, Col. Norman S. and CWO2 Mark J. Denger. "The Creation of the National Guard of California," The California State Military Museum at http://www.militarymuseum.org/CreationNGC.html : accessed 28 July 2006.

McCain, Paul Moffatt. *The County Court in North Carolina Before 1750*. Durham, North Carolina: Duke University Press, 1954.

Meier, Judith Ann. "The Federal Direct Tax of 1798: The Window Pane Tax," Bulletin of HSMC, published by the Historical Society of Montgomery County, Pennsylvania, Vol. 22, page 358.

Nankivell, John H., Maj. *History of the Military Organizations of the State of Colorado, 1860-1935*. Denver, Colorado: W.H. Kistler Stationery Co., 1935.

Norris, David A., "Revenue Stamps and Civil War," *Military Images*, May/June 1999, http://www.findarticles.com/p/articles/mi_qa3905/is_199905/ai_n8829225 : accessed 5 December 2005.

Ogden, Frederic D. *The Poll Tax in the South*. University, Alabama: University of Alabama Press, 1958.

"Poll Books," Research Notes No. 6, Library of Virginia website http://www.lva.lib.va.us/whatwehave/gov/va6_pollbooks.htm.

Ratner, Sidney, *Taxation and Democracy in America*. New York: John Wiley & Sons, 1967. Reprint: New York, Octagon Books, 1980.

Ratner, Sidney. *American Taxation: Its History as a Social Force in Democracy*. New York: W.W. Norton & Company, Inc., 1942.

Richards, Leonard L. *Shays's Rebellion: The American Revolution's Final Battle*. Philadelphia: University of Pennsylvania Press, 2002.

Ripley, William Zebina, *The Financial History of Virginia, 1609-1776*, Studies in History, Economics and Public Law, Vol. IV, No. 1, New York: Columbia College, 1893.

Rose, Christine. *Courthouse Research for Family Historians*. San Jose, California: Rose, 2004.

Rose, Richard. *The International Encyclopedia of Elections*. Washington, D.C.: Congressional Quarterly, Inc., 2000.

Shurtleff, Nathaniel B., editor. *Records of the Governor and Company of the Massachusetts Bay in New England*, 5 vols. Boston: 1853-54.

Sperry, Kip. *Reading Early American Handwriting*. Baltimore: Genealogical Publishing Co., 1998.

Spofford, A. R. "Homestead and Exemption Laws," *Cyclopaedia of Political Science*. Maynard, Merrill, and Co. 1899. Ed. John Joseph Lalor. Library of Economics and Liberty. http://www.econlib.org/library/ YPDBooks/Lalor/llCy544.html : accessed 29 May 2005.

Swierenga, Robert P. *Acres for Cents: Delinquent Tax Auctions in Frontier Iowa*. Westport, Connecticut: Greenwood Press, 1976.

Tax History Museum at http://www.tax.org/Museum/1777-1815.htm : accessed 12 December 2005.

Thompson, Sr., Milton D. "Kentucky Tax Lists Have Useful Information." *Bluegrass Roots*, Fall 1985.

Thorndale, William and William Dollarhide. *Map Guide to the U.S. Federal Censuses, 1790-1920*. Baltimore: Genealogical Publishing Co., Inc., 1987.

U.S. History.com, http://www.u-s-history.com/pages/h363.html : accessed 6 January 2006.

Webber, Carolyn and Aaron Wildavsky. *A History of Taxation and Expenditure in the Western World*. New York: Simon and Schuster, 1986.

West, Max, *The Inheritance Tax*. Clark, New Jersey: The Lawbook
Exchange, Inc., 2003. Originally published in Studies in History,
Economics, and Public Law; vol. 4, no. 2. New York: Columbia
College, 1893.

Winslow, Jr., Raymond A. "Chapter 14: Tax and Fiscal Records," *North
Carolina Research, Genealogy and Local History*. Helen Leary, editor.
Raleigh, North Carolina: North Carolina Genealogical Society, 1996.

Bibliography of Selected Tax Records

An Index to Georgia Tax Digests, 1789-1817, 5 Volumes. Spartanburg, S.C.: The Reprint Company, 1986.

Apple Press, abstractors. *The First Tax List for the Province of Pennsylvania and the Three Lower Counties, 1693*. Bedminster, Pennsylvania: Adams Apple Press, 1994.

Bendler, Bruce A. *Colonial Delaware Records, 1681-1713*. Westminster, Maryland: Family Line Publications, 1990.

Buck, Clifford M., Arthur and Nancy Kelly, editors. *Dutchess County, NY, Tax Lists 1718-1787 with Rombout Precinct by William Willis Reese*. Rhinebeck, NY: Kinship, 1990.

Certificates of Head Tax Paid by Aliens Arriving at Seattle from Foreign Contiguous Territory, 1917-1924, NARA Publication RG 85, M1365, Introduction. Washington, D.C.: National Archives, roll 1.

Civil War Direct Tax Assessment Lists: Tennessee (6 rolls), RG T227. National Archives.

Dumont, William H., editor. *Tax Lists, Westmoreland County, Pennsylvania, 1786-1810*. Washington, D.C.: National Genealogical Society, 1968.

Georgia. District 4. Internal Revenue Lists for Georgia, 1865-66 and Monthly and Special Lists, 1866. RG 58, M762. Washington, D.C.: National Archives.

Hicks, Theresa M. and Frances S. Osburn, editors. *South Carolina Quitrents, 1772-1773-1774*. Columbia, South Carolina: Peppercorn Publications, 1998.

Hill, Don Gleason, editor. *Early Records of the Town of Dedham, Massachusetts, 1636-1659*. Dedham, Mass.: Office of the Dedham Transcript, 1892.

Horvath, Jr., George J. *The Particular Assessment Lists for Baltimore and Carroll Counties, 1798*. Silver Spring, Maryland: Family Line Publications, 1986.

McNealy, Terry A. and Waite, Frances Wise, editors. *Bucks County, Pennsylvania, Tax Records, 1693-1778*. Doylestown, Pa.: Bucks County Genealogical Society, 1982.

North Carolina. *Chowan County. Chowan County, North Carolina, 1717 Tax Listing.* Signal Mountain, Tenn.: Mountain Press, 199-204.

North Carolina. *Edgecombe County Superior Court. Inheritance Tax Records, 1920-1961.* North Carolina Department of Archives and History. Microfilm no. 0,370,226, Family History Library, Salt Lake City, Utah.

North Carolina. *Franklin County. Inheritance Tax Records, 1920-1964.* Microfilm no. 0,427,266. Family History Library. Salt Lake City, Utah.

Pennsylvania. Allegheny County. *A General List of Taxables in Allegheny County, Pennsylvania, September 22, 1794.* Microfilm no. 1,698,071, Item 35, Family History Library. Salt Lake City, Utah.

Pennsylvania. *Allegheny County. Tax and Exoneration Lists, 1791.* Microfilm no. 0,295,759, Item 1. Family History Library, Salt Lake City, Utah.

Pennsylvania. Philadelphia County. *Proprietary tax list of Philadelphia County & City, 1769, pertaining to the inhabitants of Philadelphia County (including that area which became Montgomery County in 1784) and the City of Philadelphia.* Reprinted from the Pennsylvania Archives, Series 3, Vol. 14. Westminster, Maryland: Family Line Publications, 1988.

Pennsylvania. *Westmoreland County. Tax and Exoneration Lists, 1783-86.* Microfilm no. 1,027,065, Item 2. Family History Library. Salt Lake City, Utah.

Pennsylvania. *Westmoreland County. Tax Lists, 1787-1794.* Microfilm no. 1,027,066. Family History Library. Salt Lake City, Utah.

Prichard, Katharine A. *Proprietors' Records of the Town of Waterbury, Connecticut, 1677-1761.* Waterbury, Connecticut: The Mattatuck Historical Society, 1911.

Smith, Annie Laurie Wright. *The quit rents of Virginia. Copy of the rent rolls of the sevll countys in Virginia for the year 1704 referred to in Col. Nicholsons Lre: of the 25th July last. And land owners of that section called the Northern Neck; no quit rents exist.* Virginia: Wright, 1957.

T.L.C. Genealogy. *Amelia County, Virginia Tax Lists, 1736-1764: An Every Name Index.* Miami Beach, Florida: T.L.C. Genealogy, 1993.

U.S. Direct Tax of 1798: Tax Lists for the State of Pennsylvania (24 rolls). RG 58, M372. National Archives. No other state records available from NARA.

Virginia. *Tithable List for Amelia County, Virginia, 1756, Thomas Tabb's District.* The Library of Virginia, Virginia Series 07780, Roll 1116.

White, Gifford, compiler. *The 1840 Census of the Republic of Texas,* 2 vol. Nacogdoches, Texas: G. White, 1983.

Whiteside, Dora M., compiler. *Arizona Territorial Poll Tax Records, 1873-1876, Yavapai County, Prescott, Arizona.* Prescott, Arizona: Whiteside, 1984.

Woodson, Robert F., and Isobel B. Woodson. *Virginia Tithables from Burned Record Counties: Buckingham, 1773-74; Gloucester, 1770-71, 1774-75; Hanover, 1763 and 1770; James City, 1768-69; Stafford, 1768 and 1773.* Richmond, Virginia: I.B. Woodson, 1970.

Index

16th Amendment, 94, 109
24th Amendment, 49
ad valorem tax, 155
Arlington House, 103–4
assessment, 5, 85, 95, 103, 105, 114
business licenses, 100, 104, 105, 107, 133
calculating tax, 28, 34
capitation tax. *See* poll tax
carriage tax, 23, 30, 87, 89, 100, 104, 105
chartered colonies, 64
children in tax records, 20, 23, 78, 87, 118, 135, 141
Civil Rights Act of 1964, 49
Collection of Direct Taxes in the Insurrectionary Districts within the United States, 94, 101
commodities, 33, 107
county formation, 12–13
courthouse research, 10–11
deaf and dumb persons, 78
defaulter. *See* tax defaulter
direct tax, 93, 109
Direct Tax of 1798, 94–99, 111–12
Direct Tax of 1813 and 1815, 100
Direct Tax of 1861, 94, 100–103, 145
ecclesiastical tax, 132–33
estate tax, 117–27, 155
excise tax, 107, 110, 114, 134, 155
executor, 155
faculty tax, 133, 155
Family History Library, 8, 9, 139
federal tax, 93–114
free persons of color, 48, 78
gift tax, 122
handwriting, 25
head tax. *See* poll tax
headrights, 65, 66, 77, 155

homestead exemption, 37, 90–91
hypothesis, forming, 27, 38, 71, 77, 125
immigrants, 21, 59, 135
immigration, 17, 66, 135
import duties, 93, 99, 155
income tax, 94, 104–6, 109
indentured servants, 19, 44, 51, 54, 65
indexes, 15–16
inheritance tax, 117–27, 151, 155, 156
internal revenue assessment lists, 1862-1874, 149
land descriptions, 69
land tax, 20, 156
    based on quality, 24, 65
    delinquent, 37, 73–75
landless ancestor, 57
legacy tax, 117, 156
liquor taxes, 134
memorial, 5, 65, 156
migration trail, xiv, 75
migration trails, 130
military bounty land, 15
militia service, 78, 127–30
occupations, 78
old age assistance tax, 136–39, 153
personal property tax, 20, 81–93, 156
poll books, 47
poll tax, 19, 41–59, 156
    as census replacement, 59
    on women, 49
    to disenfranchise voters, 48
poll tax, 155
probate, 151, 156
probate fee, 117, 118
proprietary colonies, 65
quitrents, 64, 65, 66, 156

rate, 5, 23, 24, 33, 44, 64, 95, 101, 105, 117, 119, 120, 133, 156
real estate tax. *See* land tax
research techniques, 19–38
Revolutionary War pension application, 28, 73
road orders, 130
royal colonies, 66
school tax, 135
poor schools, 78
Shays's Rebellion, 110
slaves, 5, 16, 19, 44, 48, 51, 54, 82, 84, 87, 88, 94, 95, 100, 106, 108
Sr. and Jr., 25
state archives, 9, 10, 109, 138, 139
state income tax, 89
succession tax, 117, 155, 156
Supreme Court, 49
tariff, 93, 99, 109, 156

tax assessors, 78, 113–14
tax collectors, 113–14
tax defaulter, 7, 46, 75, 155
tax exemptions, 65, 67, 68
homestead exemption, 90–91
tax farmer, 156
tax process, 4–8
tax protests, 110–13
tax records
as census substitute, 41
tax-supported churches. *See* ecclesiastical tax
tithables, 5, 44–47, 156
tithe, 65, 156
U.S. Constitution, 49, 93, 94, 102, 109, 128
Virginia Company, 63
Virginia Military District, 15
Whiskey Rebellion, 110, 134

ABOUT THE AUTHORS

Carol Cooke Darrow, CG^{SM}, is a certified genealogist. Her interest in researching tax records grew out of her research into Virginia tithable records, which are useful in identifying the ages of male ancestors. Her research spread to North Carolina, Georgia, and Arkansas, as she developed research techniques to locate ancestors and verify family connections through tax records. She teaches and lectures in Denver, Colorado.

Susan Winchester, Ph.D., CPA, has been researching her family since 1992, tracking them from New England across the Upper Midwest to the West Coast. She became interested in historical tax records while studying at the University of Denver's Graduate Tax Program. She is a volunteer at a local Family History Center.

www.ingramcontent.com/pod-product-compliance
Lightning Source LLC
Chambersburg PA
CBHW072241270326
41930CB00010B/2222

9780788442988